FAMILY ALBUM
OF
Knits

EDITED BY BOBBIE MATELA

HOUSE of
WHITE
BIRCHES

PUBLISHERS
SINCE 1947

FAMILY ALBUM OF KNITS™

EDITOR	Bobbie Matela
ART DIRECTOR	Brad Snow
PUBLISHING SERVICES MANAGER	Brenda Gallmeyer
ASSOCIATE EDITORS	Kathy Wesley, Dianne Schmidt
ASSISTANT ART DIRECTOR	Nick Pierce
COPY SUPERVISOR	Michelle Beck
COPY EDITORS	Beverly Richardson, Kim English
GRAPHIC ARTS SUPERVISOR	Ronda Bechinski
GRAPHIC ARTIST	Nicole Gage
PRODUCTION ASSISTANTS	Cheryl Kempf, Marj Morgan
TECHNICAL ARTISTS	Nicole Gage, Leigh Maley
TECHNICAL EDITOR	Charlotte Quiggle, Diane Zangl
PHOTOGRAPHY	Tammy Christian, Don Clark, Matthew Owen, Jackie Schaffel
PHOTO STYLISTS	Tammy Nussbaum, Tammy M. Smith
PUBLISHING DIRECTOR	David J. McKee
EDITORIAL DIRECTOR	Gary Richardson
MARKETING DIRECTOR	Dan Fink

Printed in China

Hardcover ISBN-10: 1-59217-104-4 Hardcover ISBN-13: 978-1-59217-104-0
Softcover ISBN-10: 1-59217-109-5 Softcover ISBN-13: 978-1-59217-109-5
First Printing: 2006
Library of Congress Control Number: 2005933232

Every effort has been made to ensure the accuracy and completeness of the instructions in this book. However, we cannot be responsible for human error, for the results when using materials other than those specified in the instructions or for variations in individual work.

1 2 3 4 5 6 7 8 9

WELCOME

Fill your family album with knitted creations that will become treasured memories.

A lovingly made garment knit just for you or your child can evoke warm thoughts of the person who made it or of events that happened while wearing it. Items knit to decorate a home can transform it into a uniquely comforting backdrop for living, loving and taking photos to record it all. Pets that are a part of our life can turn us into doting pet parents who enjoy knitting for and photographing our four-legged family members.

We've chosen projects for this book with family members and events in mind.

The Babyhood chapter offers a wardrobe of options for little ones along with a sweater for the new mommy.

In the School Years chapter you'll find kid and teen-style sweaters, bags for books or laptops, and afghans that will comfort college freshmen during the first days away from home.

Create knitted fashions that will be cause for photo opportunities at Family Reunion time. This chapter includes coordinated styles for the whole family.

Whether you are decorating a new house, updating your current home or making a wedding gift, find the look you desire in the House Becomes Home chapter.

Make sure your pets are comfy with warm coats and cushy beds. The Pampered Pets chapter even includes pet toys.

To prepare for the holiday season, spend some time making clever tree ornaments and stockings from the Christmas Time chapter. Then choose from a wonderful selection of quick gifts that will leave you time to make sure your camera is handy to capture the most festive and touching scenes.

The Plymouth Yarn Company yarns made it easy to make each design worthy of our *Family Album of Knits*.

With warm thoughts,

Bobbie Matela

❧ CONTENTS ☙

House Becomes Home

Pampered Pets

Christmas Time

❧ BABYHOOD ❧

*From wonderful sweaters
for a new baby to wear home
from the hospital to fashions
for active babies and toddlers,
we have it covered.*

Welcome Home Trio

DESIGNS BY KATHY SASSER

Size

Newborn to 3 months (3–6 months) Instructions are given for smallest size, with larger size in parentheses. When only 1 number is given, it applies to both sizes.

Finished Measurements

Sock heel to toe: 3 (3½) inches
Bonnet around face: 10 (12) inches
Blanket: Approx 21 x 27 inches

Materials

- Plymouth Wildflower D.K. 51 percent cotton/49 percent acrylic DK weight yarn (136 yds/50g per ball): Bonnet and Socks: 1 ball each; Blanket: 6 balls pink #53
- Size 3 (3.25mm) double-pointed needles or size needed to obtain sock gauge
- Size 5 (3.75mm) 16-, 24-, and 39-inch circular needles or size needed to obtain bonnet and blanket gauges
- Stitch markers
- Stitch holder
- Cable needle
- 1 (⅜-inch) button

Gauge

Socks: 24 sts and 36 rows = 4 inches/10 cm in St st with smaller needles
Bonnet: 24 sts and 32 rows = 4 inches/10cm in St st with larger needle
Blanket: 26 sts and 32 rows = 4 inches/10 cm in Cable Seed pat with larger needle

To save time, take time to check gauge.

Special Abbreviations

C4B (Cable 4 Back): Sl 2 sts to cn and hold in back, k2, k2 from cn.
M1 (Make 1): Make a backward loop and place on RH needle.

Pattern Stitches

A. Double Moss (when worked in rnds with multiple of 4 sts)
Rnds 1 and 2: *K2, p2; rep from * around.
Rnds 3 and 4: *P2, k2; rep from * around.
Rep Rnds 1–4 for pat.

This dainty set is perfect for Baby's first trip home from the hospital.

B. Double Moss (when worked in with multiple of 4 sts + 2)
Row 1 (RS): K2, *p2, k2; rep from * across.
Row 2: P2, *k2, p2; rep from * across.
Row 3: Rep Row 2.
Row 4: Rep Row 1.
Rep Rows 1–4 for pat.

C. Cable Seed (multiple of 12 sts + 4)
Row 1 (WS): Purl.
Row 2: *C4B; rep from * across.
Row 3: Purl.
Row 4: *K4, [k1, p1] 4 times; rep from * to last 4 sts, k4.
Row 5: *P4, [k1, p1] 4 times; rep from * to last 4 sts, p4.
Row 6: *C4B, [p1, k1] 4 times; rep from * to last 4 sts, C4B.
Row 7: *P4, [p1, k1] 4 times; rep from * to last 4 sts, p4.
Rows 8–11: Rep Rows 4–7.
Row 12: Knit.
Rep Rows 1–12 for pat.

D. 2/2 Rib (multiple of 4 sts + 2)
Row 1 (RS): K2, *p2, k2; rep from * across.
Row 2: P2, *k2, p2; rep from * across.
Rep Rows 1–2 for pat.

Socks
Note: *Circular needle is used when working blanket to accommodate large number of sts. Do not join; work in rows.*

Cuff
Cast on 24 (28) sts. Join without twisting, pm between first and last st.
Work even in Double Moss pat for 16 (18) rnds.
Knit 4 rnds.

Beg heel flap
Knit 6 (7) sts, turn, purl these 6 (7) sts and the next 6 (7) sts. (12, 14 sts)
Place rem sts on 2 needles for instep.

Working back and forth on heel flap sts only, and slipping first st purlwise on each row, work even in St st for 1 (1¼) inches, ending with a WS row.

Turn heel
Size newborn–3months only
Row 1: Sl 1, k6, k2tog, k1, turn.
Row 2: Sl 1, p3, p2tog, p1, turn.
Row 3: Sl 1, k4, k2tog, k1, turn.
Row 4: Sl 1, p5, p2tog, p1. (8 sts)
Size 3–6 months only
Row 1: Sl 1, k8, k2tog, k1, turn.
Row 2: Sl 1, p5, p2tog, p1, turn.
Row 3: Sl 1, k6, k2tog, k1, turn.
Row 4: Sl 1, p7, p2tog, p1, turn. (10 sts)

Beg instep
Place 12 (14) instep sts on 1 needle. Knit across 8 (10) heel sts and with same needle, pick up and knit 6 (8) sts along left side of heel. (Needle 1)
Knit across 12 (14) instep sts. (Needle 2)
Pick up 6 (8) sts along right side of heel, then knit 4 (5) heel sts. (Needle 3)
Mark center of heel as beg of rnd; sts are distributed as follows: 10 (13) sts on each of needles 1 and 3, 12 (14) sts on needle 2. (32, 40 sts)
Knit 1 rnd.

Shape gusset
Next rnd: Knit to last 3 sts on needle 1, k2tog, k1; knit across sts on needle 2; k1, ssk, knit to end of needle 3.
Knit 1 rnd.
Rep last 2 rnds until 24 (28) sts rem.
Knit 9 (11) rnds.

Shape toe

Next rnd: Knit to last 3 sts on needle 1, k2tog, k1; k1, ssk, knit to last 3 sts, k2tog, k1 on needle 2; K1, ssk, knit to end on needle 3. (20, 24 sts)

Knit 1 rnd.

Rep last 2 rnds until 12 (16) sts rem.

Knit to end of needle 1, place sts from needle 3 onto needle 1.

Cut yarn, leaving a 12-inch tail.

Weave toe using Kitchener st. (For Kitchener st, see general instructions on page 161)

Bonnet

With larger 16-inch circular needle, cast on 64 (76) sts.

Work Rows 1–12 of Cable Seed pat.

Rep Rows 1 and 2.

Purl 1 row. Pm at each end of this row to indicate fold line for brim.

Work even in 2/2 Rib for 5 rows, dec 4 sts evenly on last row. (60, 72 sts)

Beg with a knit row, work even in St st until bonnet measures 6 (6½) inches from cast-on edge, ending with a WS row.

Shape crown

Row 1 (RS): K5, *k2tog, k5; rep from * to last 6 (4) sts, k2tog, k4 (2). (52, 62 sts)

Row 2 and all WS rows: Purl.

Row 3: K4, *k2tog, k4; rep from * to last 6 (4) sts, k2tog, k4 (2). (44, 52 sts)

Row 5: K3, *k2tog, k3; rep from * to last 6 (4) sts, k2tog, k4 (2). (36, 42 sts)

Row 7: K2, *k2tog, k2; rep from * to last 2 sts, k2tog (k2). (27, 32 sts)

Row 9: K1, *k2tog, k1; rep from * to last 2 sts, k2tog (k2). (18, 22 sts)

Row 11: *K2tog across. (9, 11 sts)

Row 12: Purl.

Cut yarn leaving an 18-inch tail. Draw yarn through rem sts twice and pull tightly.

Beg at crown, sew back seam for 2¼ (2½) inches.

Turn brim to outside along seam line. Sew ends of brim to side edges of bonnet.

Beg strap

Mark right bonnet brim ¼ inch from bottom edge. Place 2nd marker 1 inch from first.

With smaller needles and RS facing, pick up and knit 6 sts between markers.

Beg with Row 2, work even in Double Moss pat until 9 (10) reps have been completed, ending with Row 4 of pat.

Buttonhole row: K2, bind off next 2 sts, k2.

Next row: P2, cast on 2 sts, p2.

Work 1 more row of pat.

Bind off in pat.

Sew on button.

Blanket

With 24-inch circular needle, cast on 126 sts.

Set up pat

Row 1 (WS): K1, purl to last st, k1.

Row 2: P1, *C4B; rep from * to last st, p1.

Keeping 1 st at each end in rev St st and rem sts in Cable Seed pat, work in established pat until 17 reps of Cable Seed pat have been completed.

Rep Rows 1 and 2.

Do not bind off, sl sts to longer needle.

Beg border

Pm, pick up and knit 1 st in corner, pm; pick up and knit 168 sts along side edge; pm, pick up and knit 1 st and pm for 2nd corner; pick up and knit 126 sts along cast on edge; pm, pick up and knit 1 st and pm for 3rd corner; pick up and knit 168 sts along side edge, pm, pick up and knit 1 st and pm for last corner. Join for working in the round. (592 sts)

Set up pat

Rnd 1: *Work in pat to marked st, M1, knit marked st, M1; rep from * around.

Rnd 2: Work even in pat, keeping marked corner sts in knit and working new sts into pat.

[Rep last 2 rnds] 3 times more. (624 sts)

Bind off loosely in pat. ◆

DESIGNS BY ANITA CLOSIC & JOANNE TURCOTTE

Future Star

Size

Infant/child's 6–12 months (18–24 months, 2–4 years) Instructions are given for smallest size, with larger sizes in parentheses. When only 1 number is given, it applies to all sizes.

Finished Measurements

Chest (buttoned): 25 (28, 31) inches
Length: 11½ (12½, 14½) inches
Hat circumference: 14 (16, 18) inches

Materials

- Plymouth Baby Rimini 85 percent acrylic/15 percent wool super bulky weight yarn (38 yds/50g per ball): 5 (6, 7) balls pink variegated #303
- Size 13 (9mm) 24-inch circular needles
- Size 15 (10mm) double-pointed, 16-, and 24-inch circular needles or size needed to obtain gauge
- Stitch markers
- Stitch holders
- 6 (1-inch) star buttons

Gauge

8 sts and 13 rows = 4 inches/10cm in St st with larger needles
To save time, take time to check gauge.

Pattern Notes

Jacket is worked from the top down.

Circular needle is used to accommodate large number of sts. Do not join; work in rows.

Inc are worked by knitting in front and back of st.

Buttonholes are worked on the right front band for girls and on the left front band for boys.

Buttonhole row (for girls): Work to last 3 sts, yo, k2tog, k1.

Buttonhole row (for boys): K1, k2tog, yo, work to end of row.

Jacket

With larger 24-inch circular needle, loosely cast on 17 (18, 21) sts.
Row 1 (WS): P3 (3, 4), pm, p2, pm, p7 (8, 9), pm, p2, pm, p3 (3, 4).
Row 2: Knit, inc 1 st each side of every marker. (25, 26, 29 sts)
Row 3: Inc 1 st in first st, purl to last st, inc 1 st in last st. (27, 28, 31 sts)
Row 4: Rep Row 2. (35, 36, 39 sts)
Row 5: Purl.
[Rep Rows 2–5] once. (53, 54, 57 sts)

Begin front bands

Cast on 3 sts at beg of next 2 rows. (59, 60, 63 sts)

Keeping first and last 3 sts in garter st for front bands, [rep Rows 4 and 5] 4 (5, 6) times, *at the same time* make buttonholes on RS row when front bands measure ½ inch and 3½ inches. (91, 100, 111 sts)

Divide for body and sleeves

Next row (RS): Removing markers, k16 (17, 19) sts, place next 18 (20, 22) sts on holder for left sleeve, knit 23 (26, 29) back sts, place next 18 (20, 22) sts on holder for right sleeve, knit to end of row. (55, 60, 67 sts)
Row 2: K3, purl to last 3 sts, k3.
Inc row: K3, knit, inc 5 sts evenly over next 49 (54, 61) sts, k3. (60, 65, 72 sts)

Keeping front bands in garter st and rem sts in St st, work even for 7 rows.

Rep inc row. (65, 70, 77 sts)

Work even until body measures 6½ (7, 8½) inches from dividing row, ending with a RS row.

Change to smaller needles and knit 4 rows.

Bind off knitwise.

Sleeves

Sl sts from 1 holder to larger needle.

With RS facing, join yarn at underarm.

Work even in St st until sleeve measures 6 (7, 8) inches from underarm, ending with a RS row.

Change to smaller needles and knit 4 rows.

Bind off.

Assembly

Sew sleeve seams.

Sew on 2 buttons for each buttonhole, having points of stars overlapping slightly.

Hat

With larger 16-inch circular needle, cast on 28 (32, 36) sts.

Join without twisting, pm between first and last st.

Work even in St st until hat measures 5 (6, 7) inches from beg.

Star buttons add a special touch to a soft jacket and hat set.

Shape crown

Beg with Rnd 3 (2, 1), and changing to dpn when necessary, work as follows:

Rnd 1: *K7, k2tog; rep from * around.

Rnd 2: *K6, k2tog; rep from * around.

Rnd 3: *K5, k2tog; rep from * around.

Rnd 4: *K4, k2tog; rep from * around.

Rnd 5: *K3, k2tog; rep from * around.

Rnd 6: *K2, k2tog; rep from * around.

Rnd 7: *K1, k2tog; rep from * around.

Rnd 8: *K2tog; rep from * around. Cut yarn leaving a 12-inch end.

Draw yarn through rem sts twice and pull tightly.

Sew 2 buttons to side of hat, having points of stars overlapping slightly. ❧

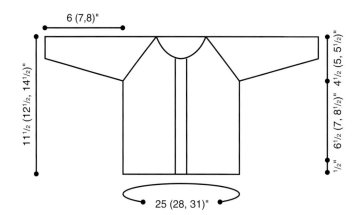

DESIGN BY SARA LOUISE HARPER

Making A Wish

Size

EASY

Child's 2 (4, 6, 8, 10) Instructions are given for smallest size, with larger sizes in parentheses. When only 1 number is given, it applies to all sizes.

Finished Measurements

Chest: 24 (26, 28, 30, 32) inches
Length: 12 (13, 14, 15, 16) inches

Materals

- Plymouth Baby Rimini 85 percent acrylic/15 percent wool super bulky weight yarn (38 yds/50g per ball): 4 (5, 5, 6, 7) balls blue variegated #305 (MC)
- Plymouth Heaven 100 percent nylon super bulky weight yarn (55 yds/50g per ball): 3 (3, 3, 4, 4) balls lilac #8 (CC)
- Size 11 (8mm) straight and 16-inch circular needles or size needed to obtain gauge
- Stitch markers

Gauge

9 sts and 16 rows = 4 inches/10cm in garter st
To save time, take time to check gauge.

Stripe Pattern

Rows 1–6: With MC, knit.
Rows 7–10: With CC, knit.
Rep Rows 1–10 for pat.

Back

With MC, cast on 27 (29, 31, 33, 35) sts.
   Work even in Stripe pat until

Comfort your child in a soft sweater that works up quickly in garter stitch.

back measures 6 (7, 7½, 8, 8) inches. Mark each end st of last row for underarm.

Continue to work even until armhole measures 6 (6, 6½, 7, 8) inches above underarm markers, ending with a WS row.

Bind off all sts knitwise.

Mark center 9 (11, 13, 13, 13) sts for back neck.

Front

Work as for back until front measures 3 (3, 3½, 4, 5) inches above underarm markers, ending with a WS row.

Shape neck

Next row (RS): K11 (11, 11, 12, 13) sts, join 2nd ball of yarn and bind off next 5 (7, 9, 9, 9) sts, knit to end of row.

Working on both sides of neck with separate balls of yarn, [dec 1 st at each neck edge every RS row] twice. (9, 9, 9, 10, 11 sts on each side)

Work even until front measures same as for back above underarm markers.

Bind off all sts knitwise.

Sleeves

With MC cast on 18 sts.

Work even in Stripe pat until sleeve measures 2 inches from

beg, ending with a WS row.

Inc 1 st each end on next and every following 6th (8th, 8th, 7th, 6th) row 5 (5, 6, 7, 9) times. (28, 28, 30, 32, 36 sts)

Work even until sleeve measures 12 (13, 14, 15, 16) inches.

Bind off loosely.

Sew shoulder seams.

Neck Band

With CC and circular needle, pick

up and knit 32 (34, 36, 38, 40) sts evenly around neck opening. Pm between first and last st.

[Purl 1 rnd, knit 1 rnd] twice.

Purl 1 rnd.

Bind off loosely knitwise.

Assembly

Sew sleeves to body between underarm markers.

Sew sleeve and side seams. ✢

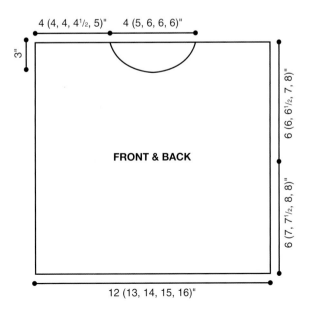

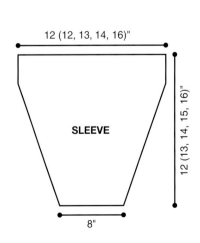

DESIGN BY ANITA CLOSIC

Nap Time Angel

Size

Approx 30 x 36 inches

EASY

Materials

- Plymouth Baby Rimini 85 percent acrylic/15 percent wool super bulky weight yarn (38 yds/50g per ball): 5 balls lilac #206 (A), 2 balls pink #203 (B)
- Size 17 (12.75mm) 32-inch circular needle or size needed to obtain gauge

6 SUPER BULKY

Gauge

8 sts and 11 rows = 4 inches/10cm in Feather & Fan pat
To save time, take time to check gauge.

Pattern Stitch

Feather & Fan (multiple of 18 sts + 6)
Row 1 (RS): With A, knit.
Row 2: K3, purl to last 3 sts, k3.
Row 3: K3, *(k2tog) 3 times, (yo, k1) 6 times, (k2tog) 3 times; rep from * to last 3 sts, k3.
Row 4: Knit.
Rows 5 and 6: With B, knit.
Rep Rows 1–6 for pat.

Pattern Note

Circular needle is used to accommodate large number of sts. Do not join; work in rows.

Blanket

Cast on 60 sts.
   Work Rows 1–6 of Feather & Fan pat 16 times.
   Work Rows 1–4.
   Bind off loosely.

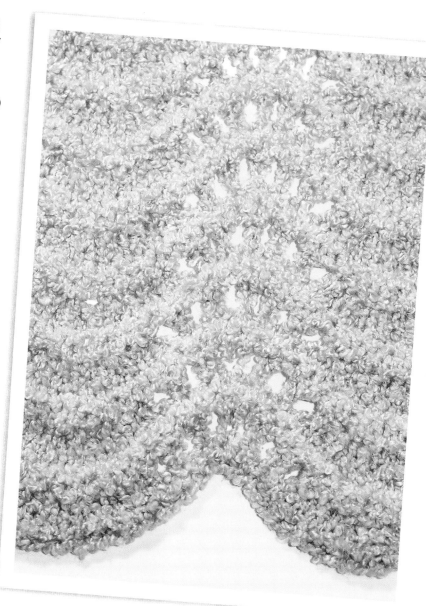

With a cuddly
blankie to hold,
your little angel
will nod off
quickly.

On-The-Go Bag & Blanket

DESIGNS BY SARA LOUISE HARPER

BAG

Size

Approx 14 inches wide
x 11 inches long x 3 inches deep

EASY

Materials

6 SUPER BULKY

- Plymouth Encore Mega Colorspun 75 percent acrylic/25 percent wool super bulky weight yarn (64 yds/100g per ball): 3 balls purple/pink multi #7135
- Size 17 (12.75mm) needle or size needed to obtain gauge
- 1 (1⅝-inch) toggle button, La Mode #31659

Gauge

7 sts and 10 rows = 4 inches/10 cm in St st
To save time, take time to check gauge.

Bag

Cast on 30 sts.
Beg with a WS row, knit 3 rows.
[Knit 1 row, purl 1 row, knit 2 rows] 3 times.
Work even in St st for 7 inches, ending with a RS row.
Knit 1 row; join a 2nd strand of yarn.

Begin base

With 2 strands of yarn held tog and working sts firmly, work even in St st for 3 inches more, ending with a WS row.
Cut 2nd strand of yarn and knit 2 rows.
Continue in St st for 7 inches, ending with a WS row.

[Knit 2 rows, purl 1 row, knit 1 row] 3 times.
Knit 3 rows.
Bind off all sts.

Handle

Cast on 7 sts.
Work even in St st until handle measures approx 45 inches.
Bind off.

Assembly

Pin handle to bag, having cast-on or bound-off edge of handle at short end of base, and long sides of handle at sides of bag.
Handle will roll naturally where not attached to bag.
Sew button to inside of bag centering it at top edge.
To close, push button through a front st.

Carry baby items easily with a quick-knit bag. It's also perfect for your knitting supplies!

BLANKET

Size
Approx 35 x 40 inches

EASY

Materials
- Plymouth Encore Mega Colorspun 75 percent acrylic/25 percent wool super bulky weight yarn (64 yds/100g per ball): 8 balls purple/pink multi #7135
- Size 17 (12.75mm) 29-inch circular needle or size needed to obtain gauge

6 SUPER BULKY

Gauge
7 sts and 10 rows = 4 inches/10 cm in St st
To save time, take time to check gauge.

Pattern Stitch
Ridges
Row 1 (RS): Knit.
Row 2: K2, purl to last 2 sts, k2.
Rows 3 and 4: Rep Rows 1 and 2.
Rows 5 and 6: Knit.
Rep Rows 1–6 for pat.

Pattern Note
Circular needle is used to accommodate large number of sts. Do not join; work in rows.

Blanket
Cast on 60 sts.
  Knit 4 rows.
  Work even in Ridges pat until blanket measures approx 39 inches, ending with Row 6 of pat.
  Knit 2 rows.
  Bind off.

DESIGNS BY SCARLET TAYLOR

Baby's First Easter

Size

Cardigan: Infant's 3 (6, 9–12, 18–24) months

Hat: Infant's 0–3 (6–12, 18–24) months

Instructions are given for smallest size, with larger sizes in parentheses. When only 1 number is given, it applies to all sizes.

EASY

Finished Measurements

Cardigan Chest: 20 (22, 24, 26) inches

Length: 8½ (9½, 10½, 12) inches

Hat Circumference: 15 (16½, 18) inches

Length: 5½ (5½, 6½) inches

Materials

- Plymouth Baby Rimini 85 percent acrylic/15 percent wool super bulky weight yarn (38 yds/50g per ball): **Cardigan:** 4 (5, 6, 8) balls yellow #202 (MC), 1 ball white #201 (CC); **Hat:** 1 ball yellow #202 (MC), few yds white #201 (CC)
- Size 13 (9mm) straight and (2) double-pointed needles
- Size 15 (10mm) needles or size needed to obtain gauge
- 1 (1-inch) button, La Mode #4764

6 SUPER BULKY

Gauge

8 sts and 12 rows = 4 inches/10cm in St st with larger needles
To save time, take time to check gauge.

Special Abbreviation

M1 (Make 1): Insert LH needle under horizontal thread between st just worked and next st, k1-tbl.

Pattern Note

Work buttonhole band on right front for girl's cardigan, and on left front for boy.

Cardigan

Back

With smaller needles and MC, cast on 20 (22, 24, 26) sts.

Work even in garter st until back measures 1 inch from beg, ending with a WS row.

Change to larger needles and St st.

Work even until back measures 7 (8, 9, 10½) inches from beg, ending with a WS row.

Shape shoulders

Bind off 3 (3, 4, 4) sts at beg of next 2 rows, then 2 (3, 3, 4) sts at beg of following 2 rows.

Bind off rem 10 sts for back neck.

Left Front

With smaller needles and MC, cast on 10 (11, 12, 13) sts.

Work even in garter st until front measures 1 inch from beg, ending with a WS row.

Change to larger needles and St st.

Work even until back measures 7 (8,

8½, 9½) inches from beg, ending with a RS row.

Shape neck

Bind off at neck edge [3 sts] once, then [2 sts] once.

Work even until front measures same as for back to shoulder.

Bind off 3 (3, 4, 4) sts at arm edge, work 1 row even, then bind off rem 2 (3, 3, 4) sts.

Right Front

With smaller needles and MC, cast on 10 (11, 12, 13) sts.

Work even in garter st until front measures 1 inch from beg, ending with a WS row.

*Baby will be the hit
of the Easter Parade
in a matching
cardigan and hat.*

Change to larger needles and St st.

Work even until back measures 7 (8, 8½, 9½) inches from beg, ending with a WS row.

Shape neck & shoulders

Bind off at neck edge [3 sts] once, then [2 sts] once.

Work even until front measures same as for back to shoulder.

Bind off 3 (3, 4, 4) sts at arm edge, work 1 row even, then bind off rem 2 (3, 3, 4) sts.

Sleeves

With smaller needles and MC, cast on 11 (13, 14, 16) sts.

Work even in garter st until sleeve measures 1 inch from beg, ending with a WS row.

Change to larger needles and St st.

Inc 1 st by M1 each end of next row, then [every 4th row] 2 (2, 0, 0) times, [every 6th row] 0 (0, 2, 1) times and [every 8th row] 0 (0, 0, 1) times. (17, 19, 20, 22 sts)

Work even until sleeve measures approx 6 (6½, 7½, 11½) inches from beg.

Bind off.

Button Band

With RS facing, using smaller needles and MC, pick up and knit 17 (19, 21, 24) sts evenly along front edge.

Knit 4 rows.

Bind off loosely.

Buttonhole Band

With RS facing, using smaller needles and MC pick up and knit 17 (19, 21, 24) sts evenly along front edge.

Mark front edge for buttonhole 1 inch below neck.

Knit 1 row.

Buttonhole row (RS): Knit to marker, k2tog, yo, knit to end of row.

Knit 2 rows, working into back of yo on first row.

Bind off loosely.

Collar

Sew shoulder seams.

With smaller needles and CC, beg and ending in picked-up rows of front bands, pick up and knit 29 sts evenly around neck.

Knit 1 row.

Row 2: K1, inc 1 by knitting into front and back of next st, k2, M1, k5, M1, k6, [M1, k5] twice, M1, k2, inc 1 by knitting into front and back of next st, k1. (36 sts)

Row 3: K1, inc 1, k4, [M1, k6] 3 times, M1, k7, M1, k3, inc 1, k1. (43 sts)

Rows 4 and 5: Bind off 1 st, work to end of row. (41 sts)

Row 6: Bind off 2 sts, k14, [M1, k3] 3 times, M1, knit to end of row. (43 sts).

Row 7: Bind off 2 sts, knit to end of row.

Bind off loosely.

Assembly

Measure down from shoulder seam 4½ (4¾, 5, 5½) inches on each side and mark.

Sew sleeves to body between markers.

Sew sleeve and side seams.

Sew on button.

Hat

With smaller needles and MC, cast on 30 (33, 36) sts, leaving a long tail for sewing seam.

Work even in garter st for 1 inch.

Change to larger needles and St st.

Work even until hat measures 4 (4, 5) inches, ending with a WS row.

Shape crown

Row 1 (RS): K2, k2tog, [k1, k2tog] 8 (9, 10) times, k2. (21, 23, 25 sts)

Row 2 and all WS rows: Purl.

Row 3 (RS): K2, [k2tog] 9 (10, 11) times, k1. (12, 13, 14 sts)

Row 5 (RS): [K2tog] 6 (6, 7) times, k0 (1, 0). (6, 7, 7 sts)

Row 7 (Size 0-3 months only): K2tog across. (3 sts)

Row 7 (Size 6-12 and 18-24 months only): K2tog, k3tog, k2tog. (3 sts)

Beg I-Cord knot

Change to CC, slip rem 3 sts onto dpn.

*K3, replace sts to LH needle; rep from * until cord measures 3 inches.

K3tog and fasten off last st.

Assembly

Tie cord into knot.

Sew back seam. 🧶

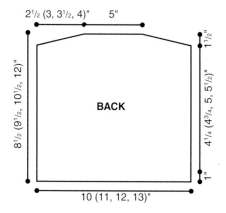

2½ (3, 3½, 4)"   5"

8½ (9½, 10½, 12)"

4¼ (4¾, 5, 5½)"

1½"

1"

BACK

10 (11, 12, 13)"

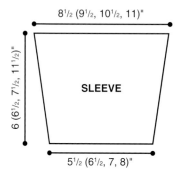

8½ (9½, 10½, 11)"

6 (6½, 7½, 11½)"

SLEEVE

5½ (6½, 7, 8)"

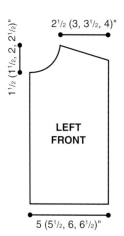

2½ (3, 3½, 4)"

1½ (1½, 2, 2½)"

LEFT FRONT

5 (5½, 6, 6½)"

DESIGN BY SCARLET TAYLOR

New Mommy Cardigan

Size
EASY

Woman's small (medium, large, extra-large, 2X-large) Instructions are given for smallest size, with larger sizes in parentheses. When only 1 number is given, it applies to all sizes.

Finished Measurements
Chest: 38 (40, 42, 46, 48) inches
Length: 21 (21½, 22½, 23½, 24) inches

Materials
- Plymouth Baby Rimini 85 percent acrylic/15 percent wool super bulky weight yarn (38 yds/50g per ball): 12 (14, 16, 16, 17) balls white #201
- Size 13 (9mm) needles
- Size 15 (10mm) needles or size needed to obtain gauge
- 3 (1-inch) buttons, La Mode #4764

Gauge
8 sts and 12 rows = 4 inches/10cm in St st with larger needles
To save time, take time to check gauge.

Special Abbreviation
M1 (Make 1): Insert LH needle under horizontal thread between st just worked and next st, k1-tbl.

Back
With smaller needles, cast on 38 (40, 42, 46, 48) sts.
Work even in garter st until back measures 1 inch from beg, ending with a WS row.
Change to larger needles and St st.

Work even until back measures 11½ (11½, 12, 13, 13) inches from beg, ending with a WS row.

Shape underarm
Bind off 4 (3, 3, 4, 4) sts at beg of next 2 rows. (30, 34, 36, 38, 40 sts)
Work even until armhole measures 8 (8½, 9, 9, 9½) inches above bound-off underarm sts, ending with a WS row.

Shape shoulders
Bind off 4 (5, 6, 6, 7) sts at beg of next 2 rows, then 4 (5, 5, 6, 6) sts at beg of following 2 rows.
Bind off rem 14 sts for back neck.

Left Front
With smaller needles, cast on 19 (20, 21, 23, 24) sts.
Work even in garter st until front measures 1 inch from beg, ending with a WS row.
Change to larger needles and St st.
Work even until front measures same as for back to underarm, ending with a WS row.

Shape underarm
Bind off 4 (3, 3, 4, 4) sts, work to end of row. (15, 17, 18, 19, 20 sts)
Work even until armhole measures 6½ (7, 7½, 7½, 8) inches above bound-off underarm sts, ending with a RS row.

Shape neckline
Bind off at neck edge [3 sts] once, then [2 sts] once.
Next row (RS): Work to last 2 sts, k2tog.
Work even until armhole measures same as for back above bound-off underarm sts.

Shape shoulder
Bind off at arm edge 4 (5, 6, 6, 7) sts twice (twice, once, twice, once), then 0 (0, 5, 0, 6) sts 0 (0, 1, 0, 1) time.

Button Band
With RS facing and smaller needles, pick up and knit 44 (45, 47, 50, 51) sts evenly along front edge.
Knit 4 rows
Bind off loosely.

Right Front
With smaller needles, cast on 19 (20, 21, 23, 24) sts.
Work even in garter st until front measures 1 inch from beg, ending with a WS row.
Change to larger needles and St st.
Work even until front measures same as for back to underarm, ending with a RS row.

Shape underarm
Bind off 4 (3, 3, 4, 4) sts, work to end of row. (15, 17, 18, 19, 20 sts)
Work even until armhole measures 6½ (7, 7½, 7½, 8) inches above bound-off underarm sts, ending with a WS row.

Shape neckline
Bind off at neck edge 3 sts once, then 2 sts once.
Next row (WS): Work to last 2 sts, p2tog-tbl.
Work even until armhole measures same as for back above bound-off underarm sts.

A cozy cardigan will keep Mommy warm, too.

Shape shoulder

Bind off at arm edge 4 (5, 6, 6, 7) sts twice (twice, once, twice, once), then 0 (0, 5, 0, 6) sts 0 (0, 1, 0, 1) time.

Buttonhole Band

Mark front edge for 3 buttonholes, placing first buttonhole 1 inch below neck edge, and rem buttonholes spaced 2 inches apart.

With RS facing and smaller needles, pick up and knit 44 (45, 47, 50, 51) sts evenly along front edge.

Knit 1 row.

Buttonhole row (RS): [Work to marker, k2tog, yo] 3 times, work to end of row.

Knit 2 rows, working into back of each yo.

Bind off loosely.

Sleeves

With smaller needles, cast on 18 (18, 20, 20, 20) sts.

Work even in garter st until sleeve measures 1 inch, ending with a WS row.

Change to larger needles and St st. Inc 1 st by M1 each end every 4th row 0 (0, 0, 0, 1) times, then every 6th row 3 (7, 7, 6, 8) times, then every 8th row 4 (1, 1, 2, 0) times. (32, 34, 36, 36, 38 sts)

Work even until sleeve measures 21 (21, 21, 21½, 21½) inches from beg.

Bind off.

Collar

Sew shoulder seams.

With smaller needles, beg and ending in picked-up row of front band, pick up and knit 31 sts evenly around neck edge.

Row 1: Knit.

Row 2 (RS): K1, inc 1 by knitting into front and back of next st, [k4, M1, k5, M1], twice, k5, M1, k4, inc 1 by knitting into front and back of next st, k1. (38 sts)

Rows 3, 5 & 7: Knit.

Row 4: K1, inc 1, k5, M1, [k6, M1] 4 times, k5, inc 1, k1. (45 sts)

Row 6: K1, inc 1, knit to last 2 sts, inc 1, k1. (47 sts)

Row 8: Ssk, knit to last 2 sts, k2tog. (43 sts)

Row 9: Bind off 2 sts, k14, [M1, k3] 4 times, M1, k15. (46 sts)

Row 10: Bind off 2 sts, knit to end of row. (44 sts)

Bind off loosely.

Assembly

Sew sleeves into armholes

Sew side and sleeve seams.

Sew buttons opposite buttonholes. ✐

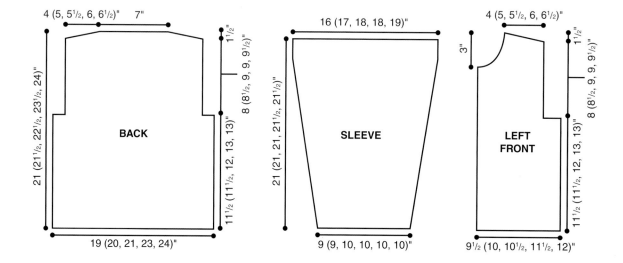

DESIGN BY CELESTE PINHEIRO

Horsin' Around

Size

INTERMEDIATE

Infant/Toddler's 12 months (18 months, 24 months, 4T) Instructions are given for smallest size, with larger sizes in parentheses. When only 1 number is given, it applies to all sizes.

Finished Measurements

Chest: 22 (24, 26, 28) inches
Length: 12 (13, 14, 15) inches

Materials

4 MEDIUM

- Plymouth Encore Worsted 75 percent acrylic/25 percent wool worsted weight yarn (200yds/100g per skein):
Boy's sweater: 2 skeins brown heather #1444 (A), 1 (2, 2, 2) skeins beige heather #1415 (B), 1 skein orange #1383 (C)
Girl's sweater: 2 skeins blue heather #149 (A), 1 (2, 2, 2) skeins pink heather #241 (B), 1 skein purple #1033 (C)
- Size 6 (4mm) needles
- Size 8 (5mm) needles or size needed to obtain gauge
- Stitch markers
- Size G/6 (4mm) crochet hook
- 4 (¾-inch) buttons

Gauge

18 sts and 23 rows = 4 inches/ 10cm in St st with larger needles To save time, take time to check gauge.

Special Abbreviation

M1 (Make 1): Make a backward loop and place on RH needle.

Pattern Stitches

Seed Stitch (even number of sts)
Row 1: *K1, p1; rep from * across.
Row 2: *P1, k1; rep from* across.
Rep Rows 1 and 2 for pat.
Seed Stitch (odd number of sts)
Every row: K1, *p1, k1; rep from * across.

Pattern Notes

When referring to chart, note that sizing for sleeves and hood are denoted with either an 'S' for sleeve or 'H' for hood. If no marking letter is present, it refers to either front or back.

Pattern is worked in intarsia method. Wind separate balls or bobbins for each color area. To avoid holes when changing colors, always bring new color up over old.

Make buttonholes on left front band for boys, and on right front band for girls.

Back

With C and smaller needles, cast on 50 (54, 58, 62) sts.

Work even in Seed st for 7 rows, ending with a WS row.

Change to larger needles.

Referring to chart on page 32 for chosen size, work even until back measures 11½ (12½, 13½, 14½) inches from beg, ending with a WS row.

Shape back neck

Next row (RS): K15 (16, 17, 18), join 2nd ball of yarn and bind off next 20 (22, 24, 26) sts, k15 (16, 17, 18).
Dec row: Working on both sides with separate balls of yarn, dec 1 st at each neck edge, purl rem sts. (14, 15, 16, 17 sts each side)

Work even until back measures 12 (12, 13, 15) inches from beg.
Bind off all sts.

Left Front

With C and smaller needles, cast on 23 (25, 27, 29) sts.

Work even in Seed st for 7 rows, ending with a WS row.

Change to larger needles.

Referring to chart on page 32 for chosen size, work even until front measures 10½ (11½, 12½, 13½) inches from beg, ending with a RS row.

A pony-look cardigan will delight the toddler in your life.

Shape front neck
Next row (WS): Bind off 5 (5, 6, 6) sts, work to end of row.

[Dec 1 st at neck edge every RS row] 4 (5, 5, 6) times. (14, 15, 16, 17 sts)

Work even until front measures same as for back to shoulder.

Bind off.

Right Front
With C and smaller needles, cast on 23 (25, 27, 29) sts.

Work even in Seed st for 7 rows, ending with a WS row.

Change to larger needles.

Referring to chart on page 32 for chosen size, work even until front measures 10½ (11½, 12½, 13½) inches from beg, ending with a WS row.

Shape front neck
Next row (RS): Bind off 5 (5, 6, 6) sts, work to end of row.

[Dec 1 st at neck edge every RS row] 4 (5, 5, 6) times. (14, 15, 16, 17 sts)

Work even until front measures same as for back to shoulder.

Bind off.

Sleeves
With C and smaller needles, cast on 32 (32, 36, 36) sts.

Work even in Seed st for 7 rows, ending with a WS row.

Change to larger needles.

Referring to chart on page 32 for chosen size, inc 1 st each end every 8th (8th, 8th, 6th) row 4 (6, 7, 9) times, working added sts into color pat. (40, 44, 50, 54 sts)

Work even until each sleeve measures 8 (9, 10, 11) inches from beg.

Bind off.

Hood
Sew shoulder seams.

With larger needles and referring to chart on page 32 for color placement, pick up and knit 54 (58, 60, 64) sts around neck.

Work even until hood measures 8 (8, 9, 9) inches above picked-up row, ending with a WS row.

Shape hood top
Pm at center of row.

Next row (RS): Knit to 2 sts before marker, ssk, k2tog, knit to end of row.

Purl 1 row.

[Rep last 2 rows] 4 times. (44, 48, 50, 54 sts)

Bind off.

Fold hood in half and sew top seam.

Front Band
With RS facing, using C and smaller needles, pick up and knit 152 (160, 176, 184) sts up right front, around hood, and down left front.

Mark front edge for 4 buttonholes, pleasingly spaced.

Work even in Seed st for 3 rows.

Buttonhole row (RS): [Work in established pat to marker, bind off next 3 sts] 4 times, work to end of row.

Next row: Working in established pat, cast on 3 sts over bound-off sts of previous row.

Work even for 2 rows.

Bind off.

Mane
With crochet hook and A, crochet a ch to measure 15 (15, 16, 16) inches, turn.

*Ch 12, sc in next ch, ch 12, sc in same ch; rep from * to end of row.

Sew mane along center top and back of hood.

Ears
Make 2.
Back
With A, cast on 7 sts. Purl 1 row.
Row 1 (RS): K1, M1, k5, M1, K1. (9 sts)
Row 2 and all WS rows: Purl.
Row 3: K1, M1, k7, M1, k1. (11 sts)
Row 5: Knit.
Row 7: K1, k2tog, k5, ssk, k1. (9 sts)

Row 9: K1, k2tog, k3, ssk, k1. (7 sts)
Row 11: K1, k2tog, k2, ssk, k1. (5 sts)
Row 13: K1, sl 1, k2tog, psso, k1. (3 sts)
Row 14: P3tog.

Fasten off last st.

Front
With B, cast on 5 sts. Purl 1 row.
Row 1 (RS): K2, yo, k1, yo, k2. (7 sts)
Row 2 and all WS rows: Purl.
Row 3: K3, yo, k1, yo, k3. (9 sts)
Row 5: Knit.
Row 7: K1, k2tog, k3, ssk, k1. (7 sts)
Row 9: K1, k2tog, k2, ssk, k1. (5 sts)
Row 11: K1, sl 1, k2tog, psso, k1. (3 sts)
Row 12: P3tog.

Fasten off last st.

With WS tog, sew front and back of ear tog along sides, leaving base open.

Sew ears to top of hood, having base open slightly so ears stand up.

Assembly
Measure 4½ (5, 5½, 6) inches down from shoulder seam on each side and place markers.

Sew sleeves to body between markers.

Sew sleeve and side seams.

Sew buttons opposite buttonholes. ❧

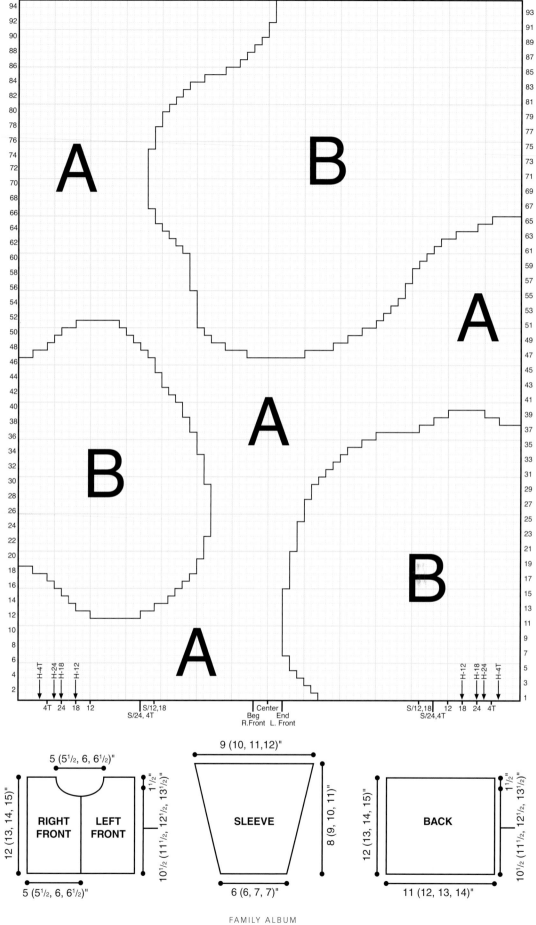

A

B

B

A

A

A

B

B

94		93
92		91
90		89
88		87
86		85
84		83
82		81
80		79
78		77
76		75
74		73
72		71
70		69
68		67
66		65
64		63
62		61
60		59
58		57
56		55
54		53
52		51
50		49
48		47
46		45
44		43
42		41
40		39
38		37
36		35
34		33
32		31
30		29
28		27
26		25
24		23
22		21
20		19
18		17
16		15
14		13
12		11
10		9
8		7
6		5
4		3
2		1

H-4T H-24 H-18 H-12

4T 24 18 12

S/12,18

S/24, 4T

Center
Beg   End
R.Front L. Front

S/12,18

S/24,4T

H-12 H-18 H-24 H-4T

18 24 4T

5 (5¹/₂, 6, 6¹/₂)"

1¹/₂"

12 (13, 14, 15)"

RIGHT
FRONT

LEFT
FRONT

10¹/₂ (11¹/₂, 12¹/₂, 13¹/₂)"

5 (5¹/₂, 6, 6¹/₂)"

9 (10, 11,12)"

8 (9, 10, 11)"

SLEEVE

6 (6, 7, 7)"

12 (13, 14, 15)"

1¹/₂"

BACK

10¹/₂ (11¹/₂, 12¹/₂, 13¹/₂)"

11 (12, 13, 14)"

DESIGN BY DIANE ELLIOTT

Baby Shower Set

Size
Newborn to 3 months

INTERMEDIATE

Finished Measurements
Chest: 16 inches
Armhole depth: 3 inches
Side to underarm: 5½ inches
Pants waist: 17 inches

Materials

SUPER FINE
- Plymouth Sockotta 45 percent cotton/40 percent superwash wool/15 percent nylon sock weight yarn (414 yds/100g per skein): 1 skein denim blues #8
- Size 3 (3.25mm) double-pointed and 16-inch circular needles or size needed to obtain gauge
- Stitch markers
- Stitch holders
- 2 (½-inch) buttons
- Size E/4 (3.5mm) crochet hook

Gauge
28 sts and 36 rows = 4 inches/10cm in St st
To save time, take time to check gauge.

Pattern Stitches
A. Seed St (even number of sts; worked in rnds)
Rnd 1: K1, p1; rep from * around.
Rnd 2: P1, k1; rep from * around.
Rep Rnds 1 and 2 for pat.
Seed St (odd number of sts; worked in rows)
All rows: K1, *p1, k1; rep from * across row.
B. 1/1 Ribbing
All rows: *K1, p1; rep from * across.

Pattern Note
Body is worked in one piece to armholes, then back and front are worked separately in rows.

Shirt
Body
With circular needle, cast on 115 sts. Join without twisting, pm between first and last st.
   Work even in Seed st pat for 10 rnds.
   Change to St st and work even until body measures 5½ inches from beg.

Divide for front and back
Knit 57 sts and place on holder for front, knit to end of rnd.

Back
Note: *Work in rows from this point.*

Shape underarm
Bind off 2 sts at beg of next 2 rows. (54 sts)
   Work even until back measures 2½ inches above bound-off underarm sts, ending with a WS row.
Dec row: K26, k2tog, k26. (53 sts)
   Purl 1 row.

Beg neck border
Row 1 (RS): K14, pm, work Seed st pat on next 25 sts, pm, k14.
Row 2: P14, work Seed st pat on next 25 sts, p14.
   [Rep Rows 1–2] 3 times more.
   Bind off all sts knitwise.

Your baby will be comfy in his fashionable denim suit.

Front
Sl front sts to LH needle; with WS facing, join yarn.

Shape underarm
Bind off 2 sts at beg of next 2 rows. (53 sts)
 Work even in St st for 3 rows.

Beg left side of neck and border
Next row (RS): K14, place rem 39 sts on holder, cast on 7 sts. (21 sts)
Row 2: K1, [p1, k1] 3 times, p14.
Row 3: K15, [p1, k1] 3 times.
 Rep Rows 2 and 3 until armhole measures same as for back above bound-off underarm sts, ending with a WS row.
 Bind off all sts knitwise.

Beg right side of neck and border
Place center 25 sts on holder.
Row 1 (RS): Working on rem sts only, cast on 7 sts, knit to end of row. (21 sts)
Row 2: P15, [k1, p1] 3 times.
Row 3: P1, [k1, p1] 3 times, k14.
 Rep Rows 2 and 3 until armhole measures same as for back above bound-off underarm sts, ending with a WS row.
 Bind off all sts knitwise.

Lower Neckband
Sl center front sts to LH needle.
 Join yarn and work even in Seed st pat for 6 rows.
Buttonhole row (RS): K1, p1, k1, yo, k2tog, work in pat to last 5 sts, ssk, yo, k1, p1, k1.
 Work 3 more rows in Seed st pat.
 Bind off all sts knitwise.
 Sew shoulder seams, matching Seed st borders.

Sleeves
With dpn, pick up and knit 45 sts evenly around armhole, including bound-off underarm sts. Pm between first and last st.
 Knit 2 rnds.

Dec rnd: K1, k2tog, knit to last 3 sts, ssk, k1. (43 sts)
 Knit 4 rnds.
 Rep last 5 rnds once. (41 sts)
 Rep dec rnd. (39 sts)
 Knit 2 rnds, decreasing one st on last rnd. (38 sts)
 Work even in Seed st pat for 5 rnds.
 Bind off knitwise.

Assembly
Tack cast-on edge of facing to inside of lower front border.
 Sew buttons opposite buttonholes.

Pants
Front
Beg at waist with circular needle, cast on 58 sts.
 Working in rows, work 1/1 rib for 4 rows.
Eyelet row: *K1, yo, k2tog, p1; rep from * to last 2 sts, k1, p1.
 Work even in 1/1 Ribbing for 4 more rows; change to St st.
 Work even until pants measure 5½ inches from beg, ending with a WS row.

Shape leg opening and crotch
Dec row: K3tog-tbl, knit to last 3 sts, k3tog.
 Purl 1 row.
 Rep last 2 rows until 26 sts rem.
 Work even in 1/1 Ribbing for 2 inches above last dec row, ending with a WS row.

Beg back
Row 1 (RS): Knit in front and back of first st, knit to last st, knit in front and back of last st.
Row 2: Purl in front and back of first st, purl to last st, purl in front and back of last st.
 Rep these 2 rows until there are 62 sts.
 Work even in St st until back measures 4¼ inches above last inc row.
 Change to 1/1 Ribbing and work even for 4 rows.
Eyelet row: K1, p1, *k1, yo, k2tog,

p1; rep from * to end of row.
 Work even in 1/1 Ribbing for 4 more rows.
 Bind off all sts.

Leg Bands
With RS facing, pick up and knit 45 sts evenly along one side of leg and crotch shaping.
 Work in Seed st pat for 5 rows.
 Bind off knitwise.
 Rep for 2nd leg opening.

Assembly
Sew side seams, including Seed st borders.

Tie
With crochet hook, make a chain approx 25 inches long.
 Beg at center front, thread tie through eyelet row at waistband.
 Tie in bow. ❧

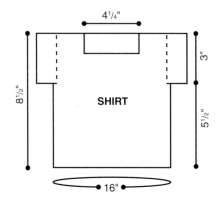

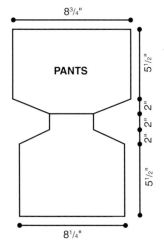

❧ SCHOOL YEARS ❧

Whether your kids are in grade school, high school or living in a dorm, they will appreciate these sweaters, book bags and afghans because they are a sign of your love.

DESIGN BY EDIE ECKMAN

Scholarship Bound

Size

INTERMEDIATE

Child's 4 (6, 8, 10, 12) Instructions are given for smallest size, with larger sizes in parentheses. When only 1 number is given, it applies to all sizes.

Finished Measurements

Chest: 27 (28½, 30, 32, 34) inches
Length: 15 (15½, 17½, 19½, 21) inches

Materials

- Plymouth Jelli Beenz 75 percent acrylic/25 percent wool worsted weight yarn (107 yds/50g per ball): 5 (6, 7, 8, 9) balls red tweed #9623
- Size 7 (4.5mm) straight and double-pointed or 16-inch circular needles
- Size 8 (5mm) needles or size needed to obtain gauge
- Stitch holders

Gauge

20 sts and 28 = 4 inches/10cm in rev St st with larger needles
To save time, take time to check gauge.

Pattern Stitch

1/1 Rib (odd number of sts)
Row 1 (WS): P1, *k1, p1; rep from * across.
Row 2: K1, *p1, k1; rep from * across.
Rep Rows 1 and 2 for pat.

Pattern Note

Inc is made by knitting in front and back of same st.

Back

With smaller needles, cast on 67 (69, 73, 79, 83) sts.

Work even in 1/1 Rib for 1½ inches, inc 1 st at center of last WS row. (68, 70, 74, 80, 84 sts)

Change to larger needles.

Beg with a purl row, work even in rev St st until back measures 9 (9, 10½, 12, 13) inches from beg, ending with a WS row.

Beg raglan shaping

Bind off 6 sts at beg of next 2 rows. (56, 58, 62, 68, 72 sts)

Dec row (RS): K1, ssk, purl to last 3 sts, k2tog, k1.
Next row: P2, knit to last 2 sts, p2.
[Rep last 2 rows] 14 (14, 16, 20, 20) times more.

Work even for 2 rows.

[Rep Dec row, work 3 rows even] 3 (3, 3, 2, 3) times.

Place rem 20 (22, 22, 22, 24) sts on holder for back neck.

Front

Work as for back, including raglan shaping, until armhole measures 4 (4, 4, 4½, 4½) inches above bound-off underarm sts, ending with a WS row.

Shape neck

Place center 10 (10, 10, 10, 12) sts on holder for front neck.

Join 2nd ball of yarn for right side of neck.

Working on both sides of neck with separate balls of yarn, continue raglan shaping as for back, *at the same time* [dec 1 st at

Your young scholar will look especially smart in this first-day-of-school pullover.

each neck edge every other row] 5 (6, 6, 6, 6) times.

Work until all raglan dec have been completed.

Fasten off last st.

Sleeves

With smaller needles, cast on 35 (37, 39, 41, 41) sts.

Work even in 1/1 Rib for 1½ inches, inc 1 st at center of last WS row. (36, 38, 40, 42, 42 sts)

Change to larger needles.

Beg with a purl row, work in rev St st, inc 1 st each side [every 6th row] 3 (4, 0, 0, 0) times, [every 8th row] 5 (5, 9, 9, 4) times, then [every 10th row] 0 (0, 0, 1, 6) times. (52, 56, 58, 62, 62 sts)

Work even until sleeve measures 10½, (12, 12½, 14, 15½) inches from beg, ending with a WS row.

Shape raglan

Bind off 6 sts at beg of next 2 rows. (40, 44, 46, 50, 50 sts)

Dec row (RS): K1, ssk, purl to last 3 sts, k2tog, k1.

Next row: P2, knit to last 2 sts, p2.

[Rep last 2 rows] 10 (14, 15, 17, 15) times more.

Work even for 2 rows.

[Rep Dec row, work 3 rows even] 6 (4, 4, 4, 6) times.

Place rem 6 sts on holder.

Assembly

Sew sleeves to front and back along raglan shaping.

Sew side and sleeve seams.

Neck Band

With dpn or smaller circular needle, knit across 20 (22, 22, 22, 24) sts of back neck, knit across 6 sts of left sleeve, pick up and knit 13 (17, 17, 17, 17) sts along left neck edge, knit across 10 (10, 10, 10, 12) sts of front neck, pick up and knit 13 (17, 17, 17, 17) sts along right neck edge, knit across 6 sts of right sleeve. (68, 78, 78, 78, 82 sts)

Pm between first and last st.

Next rnd: *K1, p1; rep from * around.

[Rep last rnd] 3 times.

Bind off loosely in pat.

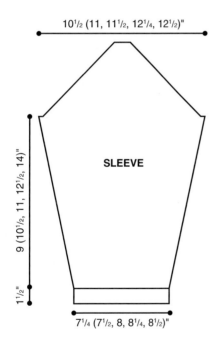

SLEEVE

10½ (11, 11½, 12¼, 12½)"

9 (10½, 11, 12½, 14)"

1½"

7¼ (7½, 8, 8¼, 8½)"

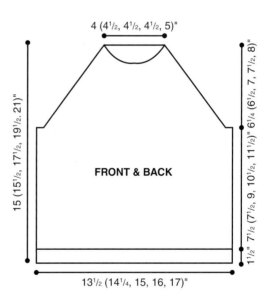

FRONT & BACK

4 (4½, 4½, 4½, 5)"

15 (15½, 17½, 19½, 21)"

6¼ (6½, 7, 7½, 8)"

7½ (7½, 9, 10½, 11½)"

1½"

13½ (14¼, 15, 16, 17)"

DESIGN BY EDIE ECKMAN

Recital Star

Size
INTERMEDIATE

Junior Girl's 1—3 (5—7, 9—11, 13—15) Instructions are given for smallest size, with larger sizes in parentheses. When only 1 number is given, it applies to all sizes.

Finished Measurements
Chest: 32 (35, 38, 40) inches
Length: 16½ (17½, 18, 18) inches

Materials
- Plymouth Firenze 40 percent nylon/30 percent wool/30 percent acrylic bulky weight eyelash yarn (55 yds/50g per ball): 5 (6, 7, 8) balls purple ombre #420

5 BULKY

- Size 13 (9mm) 16- and 24-inch circular needles or size needed to obtain gauge
- Stitch holder
- Stitch markers

Gauge
10 sts and 14 rows = 4 inches/ 10cm in rev St st
To save time, take time to check gauge.

Pattern Notes
Sweater is worked in one piece to the underarm, then divided for front and back and worked in rows. Instructions are given for knitting body in St st because knitting in the round is easier than purling. After sweater is knitted, body is turned inside out so that reverse St st is RS of fabric. Keep this in mind as you weave in ends.

Young performers will feel on top of the world in this glamorous top.

Body

With longer needle, cast on 78 (84, 90, 96) sts.

Join without twisting, pm between first and last st.

Knit every round until body measures 10 (10½, 10½, 10½) inches from beg.

Divide for front and back

Bind off 6 (6, 6, 8) sts for left underarm, k33 (36, 39, 40) sts for front and place on holder, bind off 6 (6, 6, 8) sts for right underarm, k33 (36, 39, 40) sts for back.

Back

Working in rows from this point on back sts only, work even in St st until armhole measures 6½ (7, 7½, 7½) inches above bound-off underarm sts, ending with a purl row.

Shape shoulders

Bind off 5 sts at beg of next 2 rows, then 5 (6, 7, 7) sts at beg of following 2 rows.

Bind off rem 13 (14, 15, 16) sts.

Front

Slip sts from holder onto needle.

Work even in St st until armhole measures 4 (4½, 5, 5) inches above bound-off underarm sts, ending with a purl row.

Shape neck

K12 (13, 14, 14), join 2nd ball of yarn and bind off next 9 (10, 11, 12) sts, k12 (13, 14, 14).

Working on both sides of neck with separate balls of yarn, [dec 1 st at each neck edge every other row] twice. (10, 11, 12, 12 sts on each side of neck)

Work even until armhole measures same as for back above bound-off underarm sts.

Shape shoulders as for back.

Sew shoulder seams.

Neck Band

With shorter needle, pick up and knit 46 (48, 50, 50) sts around neck. Pm between first and last st.

[Purl 1 rnd, knit 1 rnd] 3 times.

Bind off loosely.

Sleeves

Cast on 23 (25, 26, 27) sts.

Working in reverse St st, inc 1 st each end of 8th row, then [every following 6th row] 4 (0, 3, 3) times, then [every 4th row] 0 (4, 2, 2) times. (33, 35, 38, 39 sts)

Work even until sleeve measures 10 (10½, 10½, 10½) inches.

Mark each end st for underarm.

Work even for 1 (1¼, 1¼, 1½) inch more.

Bind off all sts.

Assembly

Sew sleeves into armhole, matching underarm markers to first bound-off sts of body.

Sew sleeve and side seams.

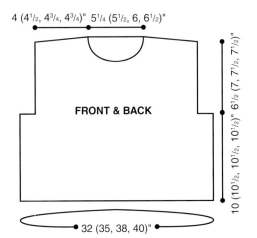

4 (4¹/₂, 4³/₄, 4³/₄)" 5¹/₄ (5¹/₂, 6, 6¹/₂)"

FRONT & BACK

6¹/₂ (7, 7¹/₂, 7¹/₂)"

10 (10¹/₂, 10¹/₂, 10¹/₂)"

32 (35, 38, 40)"

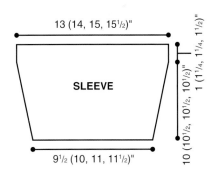

13 (14, 15, 15¹/₂)"

SLEEVE

1 (1¹/₄, 1¹/₄, 1¹/₂)"

10 (10¹/₂, 10¹/₂, 10¹/₂)"

9¹/₂ (10, 11, 11¹/₂)"

Off-To-School Bag

DESIGN BY GAYLE BUNN

Size

Approx 12½ inches wide x 13 inches high, excluding lower border

INTERMEDIATE

Materials

- Plymouth Galway Highland Heather 100 percent wool worsted weight yarn (210 yds/100g per skein): 3 skeins medium gray heather #738 (MC), 1 skein blue heather #706 (CC)
- Size 8 (5mm) needle or size needed to obtain gauge
- Cable needle
- 30 inches (1-inch wide) grosgrain ribbon to match CC
- ½ yd matching fabric
- Matching sewing thread
- 1 (1½-inch) toggle button

Gauge

18 sts and 30 rows = 4 inches/ 10cm in garter st
To save time, take time to check gauge.

Special Abbreviations

C8B (Cable 8 Back): Sl next 4 sts to cn and hold in back, k4, k4 from cn.
C8F (Cable 8 Front): Sl next 4 sts to cn and hold in front, k4, k4 from cn.

Pattern Stitch

Cable Panel (panel of 16 sts)
Row 1 (RS): C8B, C8F.
Row 2 and all WS rows: Purl.
Rows 3, 5, 7, 9 and 11: Knit.
Row 12: Rep Row 2.
Rep Rows 1–12 for pat.

Back

With MC, cast on 65 sts.
Knit 1 row.
Next row: K13, [p3, knit in front and back of next st] 3 times, p1, k13; rep from * once more. (71 sts)
Set up pat (RS): *K13, work Row 1 of Cable Panel across next 16 sts; rep from * once, k13.
Work even in established pat until back measures approx 12 inches, ending with Row 1 of Cable Panel.
Next row (WS): K13, *[p3, p2tog] 3 times, p1, k13; rep from * once. (65 sts)
Change to CC and knit 9 rows.
Bind off knitwise on WS.

Front

Work as for back.
Sew back to front along sides and across lower edge.

Lower Border

With MC and RS of front facing, working through both thicknesses of lower edge, pick up and knit 13 sts across first garter st section; [with CC, pick up and knit 13 sts across cable panel section, then 13 sts with MC in next garter section] twice. (65 sts)
Next 5 rows: K13 MC, [k13 CC, k13 MC] twice.

Shape points

Row 1 (RS): Working on first section only, ssk, k9, k2tog; turn.
Row 2 and all WS rows: Knit.
Row 3: Ssk, k7, k2tog; turn.
Row 5: Ssk, k5, k2tog; turn.
Row 7: Ssk, k3, k2tog; turn.

Row 9: Ssk, k1, k2tog; turn.
Row 10: Sl 1, k2tog, psso.
Fasten off rem st.
Rep Rows 1–10 on rem four sections.

Pompoms

Make 2 MC, 3 CC.
Referring to general instructions on page 161, make five 2-inch pompoms.
Referring to photo, sew 1 pompom to each point of lower border.

Handle

With CC, cast on 10 sts.
Row 1 (RS): Knit.
Row 2: Sl 1, k9.
Rep Row 2 until strap measures 30 inches when slightly stretched.
Bind off.
Center ribbon along WS of strap and sew in place along both long edges.

Lining

Cut 2 pieces of lining fabric, each 13 inches square.
Using ½-inch seam allowances throughout, sew side seams and bottom seam of lining.
Press top edge of lining to WS along seam allowance.

Assembly

Sew ends of handle to WS of bag at side seams, having ends overlap top border of bag.
Sew lining to inside of bag, having top edge of lining at lowest row of top border and covering ends of handles.

CONTINUED ON PAGE 53

Whether you're high school or college bound, a stylish bag is always a welcome accessory.

Jukebox Purse

DESIGN BY LINDSEY AARNESS

Size

INTERMEDIATE

Approx 8 x 10 inches, excluding strap

Materials

4 MEDIUM

- Plymouth Galway Worsted 100 percent wool worsted weight yarn (210 yds/100g per skein): 1 skein each black #09 (MC), gold #60 (A), cranberry #107 (B)
- Plymouth Galway Highland 100 percent wool worsted weight yarn (210 yds/100g per skein): 1 skein gray #702 (C)
- Size 3 (3.25mm) straight and double pointed needles or size needed to obtain gauge
- Stitch markers

Gauge

20 sts and 24 rows = 4 inches/10cm in St st
To save time, take time to check gauge.

Special Terms

Attached I-Cord

Cast on 3 sts to RH dpn. *With RS facing, pick up and knit 1 st from edge of purse, replace all sts to LH needle, pulling yarn across back of work k2, ssk; rep from * as directed. K3tog on last row.

Unattached I-Cord

Cast on 3 sts to dpn. *K3, sl sts back to LH needle; rep from * as directed. To end, k3tog and fasten off last st.

Back

With MC cast on 35 sts.
    Work even in St st until back

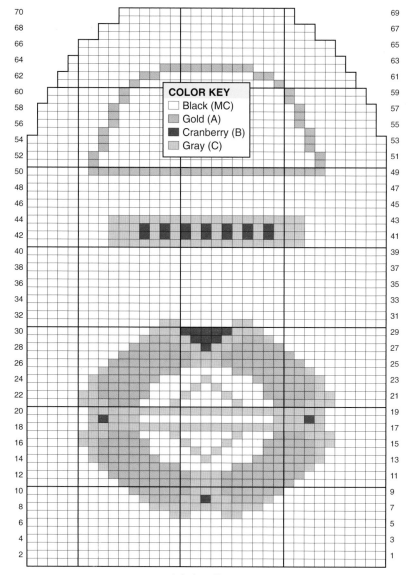

COLOR KEY
☐ Black (MC)
▨ Gold (A)
■ Cranberry (B)
▨ Gray (C)

Jukebox Purse

measures 8 inches, ending with a WS row.
    Dec 1 st each end on next RS row. Work even for 3 rows. (33 sts)
    [Dec 1 st each end every RS row]

4 times. (25 sts)
    Bind off 2 sts at beg of next 4 rows, then 3 sts at beg of following 2 rows.

CONTINUED ON PAGE 53

Take a trip back in time with a retro purse fashioned after a 1960s jukebox.

DESIGN BY DIANE ZANGL

Study Buddy Pullover

Size
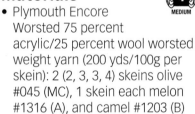
EASY

Child's 6 (8, 10, 12, 14)
Instructions are given
for smallest size, with larger sizes in
parentheses. When only 1 number is
given, it applies to all sizes.

Finished Measurements
Chest: 27 (28, 30, 32, 34) inches
Length: 14 (15½, 17, 18½, 19½)
inches.
Sleeve length: 11½ (12½, 13½, 15,
16) inches

Materials
- Plymouth Encore
Worsted 75 percent
acrylic/25 percent wool worsted
weight yarn (200 yds/100g per
skein): 2 (2, 3, 3, 4) skeins olive
#045 (MC), 1 skein each melon
#1316 (A), and camel #1203 (B)
- Size 5 (3.75mm) straight and
16-inch circular needles
- Size 6 (4mm) needles or size
needed to obtain gauge
- Stitch holders
- Stitch markers

Gauge
18 sts and 24 rows = 4 inches/
10cm in St st
To save time, take time to check
gauge.

Pattern Stitches
A. 1/1 Twisted Rib (odd number
of sts)
Row 1 (RS): K1-tbl, *p1, k1-tbl; rep
from * across.
Row 2: P1-tbl, *k1, p1-tbl; rep
from * across.

Rep Rows 1 and 2 for pat.
B. Color Stripe
Working in St st, work 2 rows each
B, A, B, then 8 rows MC.

Pattern Note
Do not cut colors; carry colors not
in use up side of work.

Back
With MC and smaller needles, cast
on 53 (53, 57, 61, 67) sts.
   Beg with Row 2, work even
in 1/1 Twisted Rib until back
measures 1½ (1½, 2, 2, 2) inches

from beg, inc 9 (11, 11, 11, 11) sts
evenly on last WS row. (62, 64, 68,
72, 78 sts)
   Change to larger needles and
St st.
   Work 6 rows in MC, then work
even in Color Stripe pat until back
measures 8 (9, 10, 11, 12) inches
from beg. Mark each end for
underarm.
   Continue to work even in Color
Stripe pat until back measures 5 (5½,
6, 6½, 6½) inches above underarm
markers, ending with a WS row.

Make this classic style using your school-aged child's favorite colors

Shape back neck and shoulders

Place center 18 (18, 20, 20, 26) sts on holder.

Working on both sides of neck with separate balls of yarn, dec 1 st at each neck edge [every row] 2 (2, 2, 3, 3) times. (20, 21, 22, 23, 23 sts rem for each shoulder)

Bind off all sts.

Front

Work as for back until front measures 4 (4½, 4, 4½, 4½) inches above underarm markers, ending with a WS row.

Shape back neck and shoulders

Place center 18 (18, 20, 20, 26) sts on holder.

Working on both sides of neck with separate balls of yarn, dec 1 st at each neck edge [every other row] 2 (2, 2, 3, 3) times. (20, 21, 22, 23, 23 sts rem for each shoulder)

Work even until armholes measure same as for back above underarm markers. Bind off all sts.

Sleeves

With MC and smaller needles, cast on 25 (25, 27, 27, 29) sts.

Work even in 1/1 Twisted Rib until cuff measures 2 (2, 2, 2½, 2½) inches from beg, inc 4 (4, 6, 6, 6) sts evenly on last WS row. (29, 29, 33, 33, 35 sts)

Change to larger needles and St st.

Work 6 rows in MC, then work in Color Stripe pat, and *at the same time,* inc 1 st each end [every 4th row] 12 (15, 15, 16, 16) times. (53, 59, 63, 65, 67 sts)

Work even until sleeve measures 11½ (12½, 13½, 15, 16) inches, ending with a WS row. Bind off all sts.

Assembly

Sew shoulder seams.

Neck band

With RS facing, using MC and smaller circular needles, knit across 18 (18, 20, 20, 26) sts of back neck, pick up and knit 14 (14, 20, 20, 20) sts along left neck edge, knit across 18 (18, 20, 20, 26) sts of front neck, pick up and knit 14 (14, 20, 20, 20) sts along right neck edge. (64, 64, 80, 80, 92 sts) Pm between first and last st.

Next rnd: *K1-tbl, p1; rep from * around.

Rep this rnd 5 (5, 7, 7, 7) times. Bind off in pat.

Finishing

Sew sleeves to body between underarm markers. Sew sleeve and side seams. ✑

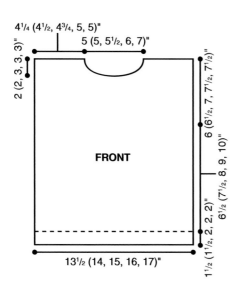

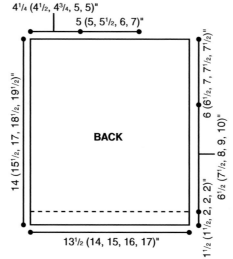

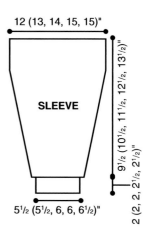

DESIGN BY SCARLET TAYLOR

Well-Connected Tote

Size
Small (medium, large)

EASY

To fit a laptop measuring approx 14 (15½, 17) inches. Instructions are given for smallest size, with larger sizes in parentheses. When only 1 number is given, it applies to all sizes.

Finished Measurements
(Before felting)
Width: 16 (16½, 18½) inches
Length: 20¾ (23¾, 25¾) inches
Depth: 3 (3½, 3½) inches
(After felting)
Width: 12¼ (12½, 14) inches
Length: 14 (16½, 17½) inches
Depth: 2¼ (2½, 2½) inches

Materials

6 SUPER BULKY

- Plymouth Yarn Hand Paint Wool 100 percent super bulky weight yarn (60 yds/100g per skein): 6 (7, 8) skeins shades of green #190
- Size 13 (9mm) needles
- Size 15 (10mm) needles or size needed to obtain gauge

Gauge
8 sts and 12 rows = 4 inches/10cm in in St st with larger needles before felting
10½ sts and 17½ rows = 4 inches/10cm in in St st with larger needles after felting
To save time, take time to check gauge.

Pattern Notes
Tote front, bottom, and back are constructed in one piece, with strap forming sides of tote.

Knit a gauge swatch using st pattern indicated. Make a note of all measurements, then felt swatch to get your felted gauge. This will also help determine amount of felting time necessary to achieve the size and look you desire.

Tote
With smaller needles, cast on 32 (33, 37) sts.

Knit 6 rows. Change to larger needles.

Work even in St st until piece measures 42½ (49, 53) inches from beg, ending with a WS row.

Knit 6 rows.

Bind off loosely.

Strap
With larger needles, cast on 6 (7, 7) sts.
Row 1 (RS): Knit
Row 2: K1, purl to last st, k1.

Rep these 2 rows until strap measures 81 (87, 91) inches from beg, ending with a WS row.

Bind off loosely.

Pocket
With smaller needles, cast on 13 (13, 16) sts.

Knit 4 rows. Change to larger needles.
Row 1 (RS): Knit.
Row 2: K1, purl to last st, k1.

Rep these 2 rows until pocket

measures 6½ (6½, 7) inches.

Bind off loosely.

Assembly
Fold tote in half and mark center 3 (3½, 3½) inches for bottom.

Sew cast-on and bound-off edges of strap between markers.

Sew sides of front and back to sides of strap.

Laptops, calculators and cell phones find a home in a sturdy, go-everywhere carrier.

Pin pocket to front of tote, centering it and having top edge 4½ (5½, 5¾) inches below top edge of tote.

Sew pocket in place, leaving top open.

Felting

Place piece in a zippered pillow protector to protect washer from felted "fuzz" or yarn fibers that accumulate during felting process, and place in top-loading washer. Set machine for smallest load size and hot water setting. To achieve best results, you want a strong agitation, so add an old pair of blue jeans to make the load a bit heavier. Add a small amount of liquid dishwashing soap; start washer and timer. Felting can take place instantly….or not, so be vigilant in watching over your project.

In approx 4–5 minutes, stop washer to check progress of felting. Remove piece from bag, squeeze out water, smooth piece and check size. Rep every 4–5 minutes, resetting machine to agitate (**DO NOT** allow to drain and spin) until piece is desired size. Remove the felted piece from its bag and rinse under lukewarm water from faucet until water runs clear. Squeeze out excess water by rolling in a towel.

Shape piece, making sure edges are straight and even. When you have achieved desired size and look, leave pieces to dry in an airy place, away from sun and direct heat. It may take several hours, or a day or two for pieces to dry completely.

DO NOT dry in a clothes dryer or further felting and shrinkage will occur. ❧

OFF-TO-SCHOOL BAG CONTINUED FROM PAGE 44

Closure

Cut 3 (10-inch) lengths of CC. Referring to page 163 make a twisted cord for toggle loop.

Attach loop to back of bag at center of top edge.

Sew toggle to front of bag. ❧

JUKEBOX PURSE CONTINUED FROM PAGE 46

Bind off rem 11 sts.

Front

Work as for back.

Referring to chart, work motifs on front in duplicate st. For instructions on how to work Duplicate st, see general instructions on page 162.

Bottom

With MC, cast on 35 sts.
Knit 10 rows.
Bind off knitwise.

*With C, pick up and knit 10 sts along one short end of bottom.
Knit 12 rows.
Bind off.
Rep from * along rem opposite end.
Pin MC of bottom to cast-on row of front. Wrap C sections up sides of purse and pin.
Sew in place.
Rep for back.

Sides

With A, work Attached I-cord around rem edges of front, beg and ending at each C side section.
Rep for back.

Join front and back

Mark top center 23 sts of I-cord for opening.

*With 1 dpn, pick up sts along edge of front I-cord, beg above C side section and ending at top marker.

With 2nd dpn, pick up same number of sts along edge of back I-cord.

With B, cast on 3 sts to 3rd needle for joining cord.

Hold needles 1 and 2 parallel to each other in LH. Sl sts from needle 3 to front needle in LH.

With B, **k1, ssk using 2nd I-cord st and first picked-up st on back needle, k2tog using 3rd I-cord st and first picked up st on front needle. Replace 3 sts to front needle and rep from ** to top marker.
Last row: K3tog, fasten off last st.*
Rep from * to * along rem side.

Strap

With A, work Unattached I-cord to measure 32 inches.

With B, work 1 row of Attached I-cord along length of I-cord just worked.

With A, work a 2nd row Attached I-cord along B.

Sew strap to sides, ending 3 inches below top opening. ❧

DESIGN BY ANITA CLOSIC

Pajama Party Throw

Size
Approx 45 x 55 inches, excluding fringe

Materials
- Plymouth Encore Mega 75 percent acrylic/25 percent wool super bulky weight yarn (64 yds/100g per skein): 4 skeins pink #137 (A), 5 skeins orange #1316 (B)
- Plymouth Hand Paint Wool 100 percent wool super bulky weight yarn (60 yds/100g per skein): 3 skeins shades of red #170 (C)
- Plymouth Jungle 100 percent nylon super bulky weight ribbon yarn (61 yds/50g per ball): 2 balls red/orange variegated #2 (D)
- Plymouth Parrot 100 percent nylon super bulky weight ribbon yarn (28 yds/50g per ball): 3 balls red/orange variegated #2 (E)
- Size 17 (12.75mm) 32-inch circular needle or size needed to obtain gauge

Gauge
8 sts and 11 rows = 4 inches/10cm in Feather and Fan pat
To save time, take time to check gauge.

Pattern Stitches
A. Feather & Fan (multiple of 18 sts + 4)
Row 1 (RS): Knit.
Row 2: K2, purl to last 2 sts, k2.
Row 3: K2, *(k2tog) 3 times, (yo, k1) 6 times, (k2tog) 3 times; repeat from * to last 2 sts, k2.
Row 4: Knit.
Rep Rows 1–4 for pat.

B. Stripe Pattern
With B, work 4 rows Feather & Fan pat.
With A, knit 2 rows.
With C, work 4 rows Feather & Fan pat.
With A, knit 2 rows.
With B, work 4 rows Feather & Fan pat.
With A, work 4 rows Feather & Fan pat.
With B, knit 2 rows.
With E, work 4 rows Feather & Fan pat.
With A, knit 2 rows.
With B, work 4 rows Feather & Fan pat.
Rep these 32 rows for Stripe pat.

Pattern Note
Circular needle is used to accommodate large number of sts. Do not join; work in rows.

Throw
With D cast on 94 sts.
Knit 1 row, work Rows 1–4 of Feather & Fan pat, knit 2 rows.
[Rep 32 rows of Stripe pat] 4 times.
Change to D and knit 4 rows.
Bind off loosely.

Fringe
Cut 6 strands each of C, D, and E, each 18 inches long.
Following Fringe instructions on page 161, make Single Knot Fringe, holding 1 strand of each yarn tog and placing knots at every scallop across cast-on edge.
Trim ends evenly.

The bright and cheery colors in this throw will add spark to any slumber party.

DESIGN BY ANITA CLOSIC

Ivy League Throw

Size

Approx 45 x 55 inches

Materials

- Plymouth Encore Worsted 75 percent acrylic/25 percent wool worsted weight yarn (200 yds/100g per skein): 6 balls olive #045 (A)
- Plymouth Rimini Rainbow 60 percent acrylic/40 percent wool super bulky weight yarn (38 yds/50g per ball): 10 balls brown rainbow #29 (B)
- Plymouth Hand Paint Wool 100 percent wool super bulky weight yarn (60 yds/100g per skein): 3 skeins red/brown multi #160 (C)
- Size 17 (12.75mm) 32-inch circular needle or size needed to obtain gauge
- Size K-10½ (6.5mm) crochet hook

Gauge
8 sts and 8 rows = 4 inches/10cm in garter st
To save time, take time to check gauge.

Pattern Stitch
Stripe Pattern
Working in garter st, knit
　6 rows B
　4 rows A (3 strands)
　4 rows C
　4 rows B
　4 rows C
　4 rows A (3 strands)
　6 rows B
Rep these 32 rows for Stripe pat.

Pattern Notes
Circular needle is used to accommodate large number of sts. Do not join; work in rows. When working with A, hold 3 strands tog.

Throw
With 3 strands of A held tog, cast on 88 sts.
　Knit 2 rows.
　[Rep 32-row Stripe pat] 5 times.
　Change to A and knit 2 rows.
　Bind off loosely.

Edging
With crochet hook, and 3 strands of A held tog, work 1 row of sc along 1 side edge; do not turn.
　Working from left to right in rev sc, work 1 sc in each sc of previous row.
　Fasten off.
　Rep along opposite side edge.

Knit a throw for your favorite college student. Easy garter stitch, large needles, and textured yarns combine for a project that will be finished in no time.

❧ FAMILY REUNION ❧

Here are picture-perfect designs that are worthy of the family reunion photo-ops. We've included coordinating sweaters for man, woman and child.

DESIGN BY KATHARINE HUNT

Dad's Easy Crew Neck

Sizes

EASY

Man's small (medium, large, extra-large, 2X-large) Instructions are given for smallest size, with larger sizes in parentheses. When only 1 number is given, it applies to all sizes.

Finished Measurements

Chest: 45 (47, 49½, 52, 54) inches
Length: 26 (26½, 27, 27½, 28) inches

Materials

4 MEDIUM

- Plymouth Galway Worsted 100 percent wool medium weight yarn (210 yds/100g per ball): 6 (7, 7, 8, 9) balls dark olive #59 (A), 1 (2, 2, 2, 3) balls medium olive #106 (B), 1 ball each blue #128 (C) and pale olive #121 (D)
- Size 5 (3.75mm) needles
- Size 7 (4.5mm) needles or size needed to obtain gauge
- Tapestry needle

Gauge

21 sts and 37 rows = 4 inches/ 10cm in pat st with larger needles To save time, take time to check gauge.

Pattern Stitch

A. Ridged Stripes (multiple of 6 sts + 4)
(Back & Sleeves)
Row 1 (RS): With A, knit.
Row 2: With A, purl.
Rows 3 and 4: With B, k4, *sl 2, k4; rep from * to end.
Rows 5 and 6: Rep Rows 1 and 2.

Rows 7 and 8: With C, k1, sl 2, *k4, sl 2; rep from * to last st, k1.
Rows 9–14: Rep Rows 1–6.
Rows 15 and 16: With D, rep Rows 7 and 8.
Rep Rows 1–16 for pat.
B. Ridged Stripes (multiple of 6 sts + 4)
(Front)
Row 1 (RS): With A, knit.
Row 2: With A, purl.
Rows 3 and 4: With B, k1, sl 2, *k4, sl 2; rep from * to last st, k1.

Rows 5 and 6: Rep Rows 1 and 2.
Rows 7 and 8: With C, k4, *sl 2, k4; rep from * to end.
Rows 9–14: Rep Rows 1–6.
Rows 15 and 16: With D, Rep Rows 7 and 8.
Rep Rows 1–16 for pat.

Pattern Notes

Carry colors not in use up side of work.

Work all edge sts in St st.

Slip stitches and garter ridges create easy textured stripes on this update of the basic pullover.

Back

With smaller needles and A, cast on 117 (123, 129, 135, 141) sts.

Row 1: K1, *p1, k1; rep from * across row.

Work ribbing as established for a total of 14 (14, 16, 16, 18) rows, inc 1 st on last row. (118, 124, 130, 136, 142 sts)

Change to larger needles, and work even in Ridged Stripe (Back version) until piece measures approx 16 (16, 16, 16½, 16½) inches from beg, ending with a WS row in B or C.

Shape armhole

Bind off 9 sts at beg of next 2 rows. (100, 106, 112, 118, 124 sts)

Bind off 1 st each end [every other row] 6 times. (88, 94, 100, 106, 112 sts)

Work even in pat as established until armhole measures 10 (10½, 10½, 10½, 11) inches, ending with a WS row.

Shape neck & shoulders

Next row: Work 30 (32, 34, 36, 38) sts, join 2nd ball of yarn and bind off center 28 (30, 32, 34, 36) sts, work to the end of the row.

Working on both sides with separate balls of yarn and maintaining pat, dec 1 st at neck edge [every row] 4 times and *at the same time*, bind off at shoulder edge [6 (7, 7, 8, 8) sts] twice, then [7 (7, 8, 8, 9) sts] twice. No sts remain.

Front

With smaller needles and A, cast on 117 (123, 129, 135, 141) sts.

Work ribbing as for back, inc 1 st on last row. (118, 124, 130, 136, 142 sts)

Change to larger needles, and work in Ridged Stripe (Front version), shaping armhole as for back.

Work even in pat as established until armhole measures 7¼ (7½, 7½, 7½, 7¾) inches, ending with a WS row.

Shape neck & shoulders

Next row: Continuing pat as established, work 34 (36, 38, 40, 42) sts, join 2nd ball of yarn and bind off center 20 (22, 24, 26, 28) sts, work to end of row.

Working both sides of neck with separate balls of yarn and maintaining pat, dec 1 st at neck edge [every row] 6 times, then [every other row] twice. (26, 28, 30 32, 34 sts rem each shoulder)

Work even until armhole measures same as for back.

Shape shoulders as for back.

Sleeves

With smaller needles and A, cast on 61 (63, 63, 65, 67) sts.

Work ribbing as for back, inc 1 st on last row. (62, 64, 64, 66, 68 sts)

Change to larger needles and work Rows 1 and 2 of Ridged Stripes pat (Sleeve version).

Setup row: With B, k2 (0, 0, 1, 2), work Row 3 of Ridged Stripes pat to last 2 (0, 0, 1, 2) sts, knit to end.

Inc 1 st each end on Row 5 of pat, then [every 4th row] 3 (3, 3, 4, 5) times, then [every 6th row] 20 (22, 22, 23, 21) times, working new sts into pat. (110, 116, 116, 122, 122 sts)

Work even until piece measures 18½ (19, 19, 19½, 20) inches from beg. Place markers at both ends.

Shape sleeve cap

Work even for 2¼ inches.

Dec 1 st each end every row 7 times. (96, 102, 102, 108, 108 sts)

With A, bind off.

Neck Band

Sew right shoulder seam.

With A and smaller needle, pick up and knit 28 (29, 29, 31, 31) sts along left neck, 20 (22, 24, 26, 28) sts across center front, 28 (29, 29, 31, 31) sts along right neck, and 41 (45, 49, 53, 57) sts across back neck. (117, 125, 131, 141, 147 sts)

Next Row (WS): P1, *k1, p1; rep from * to end and *at the same time*, dec 2 (4, 4, 4, 4) sts evenly across back neck. (115, 121, 127, 137, 143 sts)

Work even in rib as established for 10 (10, 12, 12, 14) rows. Bind off loosely in rib.

Assembly

Sew left shoulder and neck band.

Sew sleeves into armholes, aligning markers on sleeve with body underarm.

Sew side and sleeve seams. ✑

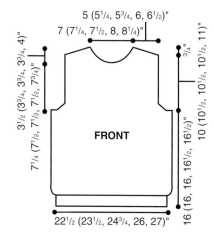

5 (5¼, 5¾, 6, 6½)"
7 (7¼, 7½, 8, 8¼)"
¾"
3½ (3¾, 3¾, 3¾, 4)"
7¼ (7½, 7½, 7½, 7¾)"
10 (10½, 10½, 10½, 11)"
16 (16, 16, 16½, 16½)"
FRONT
22½ (23½, 24¾, 26, 27)"

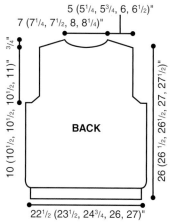

5 (5¼, 5¾, 6, 6½)"
7 (7¼, 7½, 8, 8¼)"
¾"
10 (10½, 10½, 10½, 11)"
26 (26½, 26½, 27, 27½)"
BACK
22½ (23½, 24¾, 26, 27)"

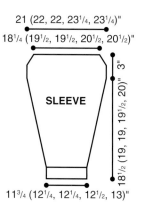

21 (22, 22, 23¼, 23¼)"
18¼ (19½, 19½, 20½, 20½)"
3"
SLEEVE
18½ (19, 19, 19½, 20)"
11¾ (12¼, 12¼, 12½, 13)"

DESIGN BY KATHARINE HUNT

Mom's Easy V-neck

Sizes

INTERMEDIATE

Woman's small
(medium, large, extra-large)
Instructions are given for
smallest size, with larger sizes in
parentheses. When only 1 number
is given, it applies to all sizes.

Finished Measurements

Chest: 36 (40½, 45, 49½) inches
Length: 22 (22½, 23½, 24) inches

Materials

MEDIUM

- Plymouth Galway
  Worsted 100 percent
  wool medium weight yarn (210
  yds/100g per ball): 4 (5, 5, 6) balls
  natural #01 (A), 1 (1, 2, 2) balls
  green #127 (B), 1 ball each aqua
  #111 (C) and pink #114 (D)
- Size 5 (3.75mm) 24-inch circular
  needle (for neck edging)
- Size 6 (4mm) needles
- Size 7 (4.5mm) needles or size
  needed to obtain gauge
- Stitch holders
- Stitch markers
- Tapestry needle

Gauge

21 sts and 37 rows = 4 inches/
10cm in pat st with larger needles
To save time, take time to check
gauge.

Pattern Stitches

A. K2, P1 Rib (multiple of 3 sts + 1)
Row 1 (RS): P1, *k2, p1; rep from
* across.
Row 2: K1, *p2, k1; rep from *
across.
Rep Rows 1 and 2 for pat.

B. Plain Ridged Stripe (multiple of 6 sts + 4)
Row 1 (RS): With A, knit.
Row 2: With A, purl.
Rows 3 and 4: With A, k4, *sl 2, k4; rep from * to end.
Rows 5 and 6: Rep Rows 1 and 2.
Rows 7 and 8: With A, k1, sl 2, *k4, sl 2; rep from * to last st, k1.
Rows 9–12: Rep Rows 1–4.
C. Colored Ridged Stripe 1
(multiple of 6 sts + 4)
Row 1 (RS): With A, knit.
Row 2: With A, purl.
Rows 3 and 4: With B, k4, *sl 2, k4; rep from * to end.
Rows 5 and 6: Rep Rows 1 and 2.
Rows 7 and 8: With C, k1, sl 2, *k4, sl 2; rep from * to last st, k1.
Rows 9–16: Rep Rows 1–8.
Rows 17–20: Rep Rows 1–4.
D. Colored Ridged Stripe 2
As Colored Ridged Stripe 1, replacing C with D.

Pattern Notes

Carry colors not in use (for each stripe) up side of work. Cut at end of stripe.

Work all edge stitches in St st.

Work decs at beg of row as k2tog; work decs at end of row as ssk.

On Front only, keep colors same as indicated, but switch stitch pattern instructions for Rows 3 and 4 with instructions for Rows 7 and 8 (see Men's pattern). This will maintain the pattern flow across the side seam.

Back

With smaller needles and C, cast on 94 (106, 118, 130) sts.

Change to A, and work K2, P1 rib for 8 rows.

Change to larger needles, and work Ridged Stripes in the following sequence:
*Plain, Colored 1, Plain, Colored 2; rep from *.

Shape sides (optional)

Work even until piece measures 4 (4, 4½, 4½) inches from beg, ending with a WS row.

Dec 1 st each end of next row, then [every 6 rows] twice. (88, 100, 112, 124 sts)

Work even for 2¾ (2¾, 3, 3) inches, ending with a WS row.

Inc 1 st each end of next row, then [every 6 rows] twice. (94, 106, 118, 130 sts)

Work even until piece measures 14 (14, 14½, 14½) inches from beg.

Shape armholes

Bind off 6 (9, 10, 13) sts at beg of next 2 rows. (82, 88, 98, 104 sts)

Dec 1 st each end of next, then [every other row] 5 (5, 7, 7) times more. (70, 76, 82, 88 sts)

Work even until armhole measures 8 (8½, 9, 9½) inches, ending with a WS row.

Shape neck & shoulders

Next row: Work 23 (25, 28, 30) sts, join 2nd ball of yarn and bind off center 24 (26, 26, 28) sts, work to end of row.

Working on both sides with separate balls of yarn and maintaining pat, dec 1 st at neck edge [every row] 4 times and *at the same time*, bind off at shoulder edge [6 (7, 8, 9) sts] twice, then [7 (7, 8, 8) sts] once. No sts remain.

Front

Note: Switch stitch patterns for Rows 3 and 4 with Rows 7 and 8 while maintaining colors (see Pattern Notes).

Work as for back until piece measures same as back to armholes, ending with a WS row. Mark 2 center sts.

Shape V-neck & armholes
Left side

Next row: Bind off 6 (9, 10, 13) sts, work to center 2 sts and put them on a safety pin, then put rem sts on holder.

Dec 1 st at armhole edge [every other row] 6 (6, 8, 8) times, and *at the same time*, dec 1 st at neck

edge [every other row] 9 (10, 10, 10) times, then [every 4th row] 3 times, then [every 6th row] 3 times. See Pattern Notes. (19, 21, 24, 26 sts)

Work even until front measures same as back to shoulder.

Bind off at shoulder edge as for back.

Right side

Join yarn at front neck edge and work to end of row.

Next row (WS): Bind off 6 (9, 10, 13) sts, work to end of row.

Dec 1 st at armhole edge on next row, then [every other row] 5 (5, 7, 7) times more, and *at the same time*, shape neck as for left side. (19, 21, 24, 26 sts)

Work even until front measures same as back to shoulder.

Bind off at shoulder edge as for back.

Sleeves

With smaller needles and C, cast on 49 (49, 55, 55) sts and work ribbing in A as for back, inc 1 st at beg of last row. (50, 50, 56, 56 sts)

Change to larger needles and work Ridged Stripes pats in same sequence as for back.

Note: *When working the first pat rep, ensure that the first st 2 in the first Row 3 of the pattern sits directly above the second k2 in the ribbing. The sleeve pattern will not necessarily be centered.*

Continue in pat as established, and *at the same time*, inc 1 st at each end of Row 3, then [every 4th row] row twice, then [every 6th row] 8 times, then [every 8th row] 6 (9, 9, 11) times. (84, 90, 96, 100 sts)

Work even until piece measures 16½ (17, 17½, 18) inches from beg. Mark ends.

Shape sleeve cap

Work even for 1¼ (1¾, 2, 2½) inches.

Dec 1 st each end [every row] 6 (6, 8, 8) times. (72, 78, 80, 84 sts)

With A, bind off.

subtle shaping at the sides gives this sweater a more feminine fit, and the V-neck is flattering on all women.

Neck Band

Sew shoulder seams.

With circular needle and A, pick up and knit 65 (69, 73, 77) sts down left front, pm, knit the 2 center sts, pm, pick up and knit 65 (69, 73, 77) sts up right front, and 40 (42, 42, 44) sts across back neck, pm to indicate beg of rnd. (172, 182, 190, 200 sts)

Next rnd: P1, *k2, p1; rep from

* to 2 sts before marker, p2tog, slip marker, k2, slip marker, p2tog, continue in rib to match previous side, and *at the same time,* dec 3 (4, 3, 4) sts evenly across back neck. (169, 178, 187, 196 sts)

Next 7 rnds: Continue in rib as established, working p2tog before and after markers as on previous rnd.

Next rnd: Change to C. Bind off in

rib, working decs before and after markers as before.

Assembly

Sew sleeves into armholes, aligning markers on sleeve with body underarm.

Sew side and sleeve seams. 🐦

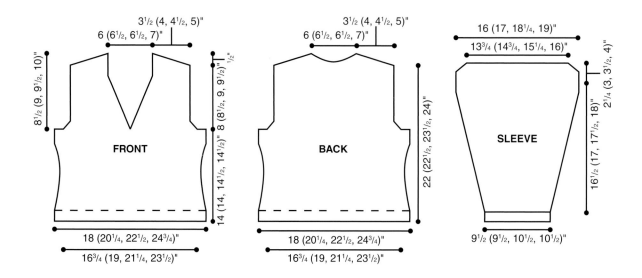

DESIGN BY KATHARINE HUNT

Brother's Easy Crew Neck

Sizes

Child's 4 (6, 8, 10) Instructions are given for smallest size, with larger sizes in parentheses. When only 1 number is given, it applies to all sizes.

EASY

Finished Measurements

Chest: 29 (31, 33½, 36) inches
Length to shoulders: 15 (16¼, 17½, 18½) inches

Materials

- Plymouth Galway Worsted 100 percent wool medium weight yarn (210 yds/100g per ball): 3 (4, 4, 5) balls blue #128 (A); 1 ball each pale olive #121 (B), medium olive #106 (C), dark olive #59 (D)
- Size 5 (3.75 mm) needles
- Size 7 (4.5 mm) needles or size needed to obtain gauge
- Tapestry needle

4 MEDIUM

Gauge

21 sts and 37 rows = 4 inches/ 10cm in pat st with larger needles To save time, take time to check gauge.

Pattern Stitch

A. Ridged Stripes (multiple of 6 sts + 4)
(Back and Sleeves; Front: see Pattern Notes)
Row 1 (RS): With A, knit.
Row 2: With A, purl.
Rows 3 and 4: With B, k4, *sl 2, k4; rep from * to end.
Rows 5 and 6: Rep Rows 1 and 2.
Rows 7 and 8: With C, k1, sl 2, *k4, sl 2; rep from * to last st, k1.

Rows 9–14: Rep Rows 1–6.
Rows 15 and 16: With D, rep Rows 7 and 8.
Rep Rows 1–16 for pat.

Pattern Notes

Carry colors not in use up side of work.

Work all edge sts in St st.

On Front only, keep colors same as indicated, but switch pattern instructions for Rows 3 and 4 with instructions for Rows 7 and 8 (see Men's pattern). This will maintain the pattern flow across the side seam.

Back

With smaller needles and A, cast on 75 (81, 87, 93) sts.
Row 1: K1, *p1, k1; rep from * across row.

Work ribbing as established for a total of 8 (8, 10, 10) rows, inc 1 st on last row. (76, 82, 88, 94 sts)

Change to larger needles, and work even in Ridged Stripe until piece measures approx 8½ (9, 9¾, 10½) inches from beg, ending with a WS row in B or C.

Shape armholes

Bind off 5 (5, 8, 8) sts at beg of next 2 rows. (66, 72, 72, 78 sts)

Bind off 1 st each end [every other row] 4 times. (58, 64, 64, 70 sts)

Work even in pat as established until armhole measures 6½ (7¼, 7¾, 8) inches, ending with a WS row.

Shape shoulders

Bind off 4 (5, 5, 6) sts at each

shoulder edge once, then 5 (5, 5, 6) sts once, and 5 (6, 6, 6) sts once. (30, 32, 32, 34 sts)

Bind off.

Front

With smaller needles and A, cast on 75 (81, 87, 93) sts.

Work ribbing as for back.

Change to larger needles, and work even in Ridged Stripe (see Pattern Notes) until piece measures approx same as back to underarms, ending with a WS row in B or C.

Shape armholes as for back.

Work even in pat as established until armhole measures 4¾ (5½, 5½, 5¾) inches, ending with a WS row.

Shape front neck & shoulders

Next row: Continuing pat as established, work 19 (21, 21, 23) sts, join 2nd ball of yarn and bind off center 20 (22, 22, 24) sts, work to end of row.

This easy knit pullover in four colors
is a pint-size version of Dad's crew-
neck sweater, using the same colors,
but switching the main color to blue.

Working on both sides of neck with separate balls of yarn and maintaining pat, dec 1 st at neck edge [every row] 4 times, then [every other row] once. 14 (16, 16, 18) sts rem each shoulder.

Work even until armholes measure same as for back.

Shape shoulders as for back.

Sleeves

With smaller needles and A, cast on 41 (43, 47, 49) sts.

Work ribbing as for back, inc 1 st on last row. (42, 44, 48, 50 sts)

Change to larger needles and work Rows 1 and 2 of Ridged Stripes pat.

Setup row: With B, k1 (2, 1, 2), work Row 3 of Ridged Stripes pat to last 1 (2, 1, 2) sts, knit to end.

Inc 1 st each end on Row 5 of pat, then [every 4th row] 6 times, then [every 6th row] 4 (6, 7, 7) times, then [every 8th row] 3 times, working new sts into pat. (70, 76, 82, 84 sts)

Work even until piece measures 11½ (12½, 14, 15½) inches from beg.

Place markers at both ends.

Shape sleeve cap

Work even for 1 inch.

Dec 1 st at each end of [every row] 7 times. (56, 62, 68, 70 sts)

With A, bind off.

Neck Band

Sew right shoulder seam.

With smaller needle and A, pick up and knit 20 (20, 24, 24) sts along left neck, 20 (22, 22, 24) sts across center front, 20 (20, 24, 24) sts along right neck, and 30 (32, 32, 34) sts across back neck. (90, 94, 102, 106 sts)

Next Row (WS): P1, *k1, p1; rep from * to end and *at the same time*, dec 3 sts evenly across back neck. (87, 91, 99, 103 sts)

Work even in rib as established for 6 (6, 8, 8) rows.

Bind off loosely in rib.

Assembly

Sew left shoulder and neck band.

Sew sleeves into armholes, aligning markers on sleeve with body underarm.

Sew side and sleeve seams.

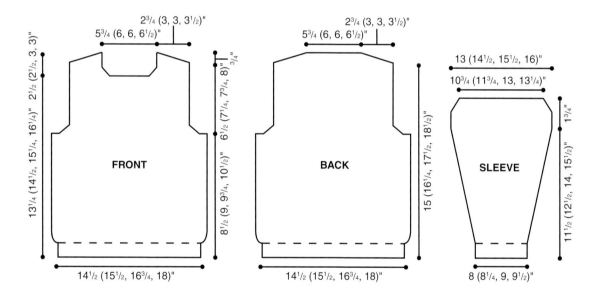

Sister's Hoodie

DESIGN BY KATHARINE HUNT

Sizes
Child's 4 (6, 8, 10) Instructions are given for smallest size, with larger sizes in parentheses. When only 1 number is given, it applies to all sizes.

INTERMEDIATE

Finished Measurements
Chest: 29 (31, 33½, 36) inches
Length: 15½ (16½, 17½, 18½) inches

Materials
- Plymouth Galway Worsted 100 percent wool medium weight yarn (210 yds/100g per ball): 4 (4, 5, 5) balls pink #114 (A), 1 ball each natural #01 (B) and turquoise #111 (C)
- Size 5 (3.75 mm) straight and 29-inch circular needles
- Size 6 (4mm) needles
- Size 7 (4.5mm) needles or size needed to obtain gauge
- Tapestry needle
- Separating zipper to fit size

MEDIUM

Gauges
21 sts and 37 rows = 4 inches/10cm in pat st with size 7 needles
20 sts and 24 rows = 4 inches in St st with size 7 needles
To save time, take time to check gauge.

Special Abbreviation
M1 (Make 1): Inc by making a backward loop over right needle.

Pattern Stitch
A. Ridged Stripes (multiple of 6 sts + 4)

(Back and Sleeves)
Row 1 (RS): With A, knit.
Row 2: With A, purl.
Rows 3 and 4: With B, k4, *sl 2, k4; rep from * to end.
Rows 5 and 6: Rep Rows 1 and 2.
Rows 7 and 8: With C, k1, sl 2, *k4, sl 2; rep from * to last st, k1.
Rep Rows 1–8 for pat.

Pattern Notes
Carry colors not in use up side of work.

Work all edge stitches in St st.

Work dec at beg of row as ssk; work dec at end of row as ssk.

Back
With size 5 needles and C, cast on 75 (81, 87, 93) sts.
Row 1 (RS): K1, *p1, k1; rep from * across.

Change to A, and work 7 (7, 9, 9) more rows in rib as established, inc 1 st on last row. (76, 82, 88, 94 sts)

Change to size 7 needles, and work even in Ridged Stripe until piece measures approx 8½ (9, 9½, 10½) inches from beg, ending with a WS row in B or C.

Shape armholes
Bind off 5 (5, 8, 8) sts at beg of next 2 rows. (66, 72, 72, 78 sts)

Bind off 1 st each end of next 4 rows. (58, 64, 64, 70 sts)

Work even in pat as established until armholes measure 6½ (7¼, 7¾, 8) inches, ending with a RS row.

Shape shoulders
Bind off 4 (5, 5, 6) sts at each shoulder edge once, then 5 (5, 5,

6) sts once, and 5 (6, 6, 6) sts once. (30, 32, 32, 34 sts)
Bind off.

Left Front
Note: On sizes 4 and 8 only-Ridged Stripes pat ends with an extra 3 sts.
With size 5 needles and C, cast on 36 (39, 42, 45) sts.

Work ribbing as on back, inc 1 st on last row. (37, 40, 43, 46 sts)

Change to size 7 needles and work Ridged Stripe pat as follows:
Rows 1 and 2: With A, knit 1 row, purl 1 row.
Row 3: With B, k1, sl 2, *k4, sl 2; rep from * to last 4 (1, 4, 1) sts, knit to end.
Row 4: With B, k4 (1, 4, 1), sl 2, *k4, sl 2; rep from * to last st, k1.
Rows 5 and 6: With A, knit 1 row, purl 1 row.
Row 7: With C, k4, *sl 2, k4; rep from * to last 3 (0, 3, 0) sts, end sl 2, k1.
Row 8: With C, [sizes 4 and 8 only: k1, sl 2], k4, *sl 2, k4; rep from * to end.

Work even in pat as established until piece measures same as back to armhole, ending with a WS row.

Shape armhole
Bind off 5 (5, 8, 8) sts at beg of next row. (32, 35, 35, 37 sts)

Bind off 1 st at armhole edge of the next 4 rows. (28, 31, 31, 33 sts)

Work even until armhole measures 6½ (7¼, 7¾, 8) inches, ending with a RS row.

Shape front neck & shoulder
Next row (WS): Bind off 3 sts at

Here's a cozy outdoor hoodie with zip front, in an easy-to-knit 3-color slip st pattern. With a change of colors, it's just right for boys as well.

beg of next row, work pat to end. (25, 28, 28, 30 sts)

Dec 1 st at neck edge [every row] 5 (6, 6, 6) times, then [every other row] row 6 times. (14, 16, 16, 18 sts)

At the same time, when armhole measures 6½ (7¼, 7¾, 8) inches, bind off 4 (5, 5, 6) sts at shoulder edge once, then 5 (5, 5, 6) sts once, and 5 (6, 6, 6) sts once.

Right Front

Note: *On sizes 4 and 8 only- Ridged Stripes pat begins with an extra 3 sts.*

With size 5 needles and C, cast on 36 (39, 42, 45) sts.

Work ribbing as for back, increasing 1 st on last row. (37, 40, 43, 46 sts)

Change to size 7 needles and work Ridged Stripe pat as follows:

Rows 1 and 2: With A, knit 1 row, purl 1 row.

Row 3: With B, k4 (1, 4, 1), sl 2, *k4, sl 2; rep from * to last st, k1.

Row 4: With B, k1, sl 2, *k4, sl 2; rep from * to last 4 (1, 4, 1) sts, knit to end.

Rows 5 and 6: With A, knit 1 row, purl 1 row.

Row 7: With C, [sizes 4 and 8 only: k1, sl 2], k4, *sl 2, k4; rep from * to end.

Row 8: With C, k4, *sl 2, k4; rep from * to last 3 (0, 3, 0) sts, end sl 2, k1.

Work even in pat as established until piece measures same as back to armhole, ending with a RS row.

Shape armhole

Bind off 5 (5, 8, 8) sts at beg of next row. (32, 35, 35, 37 sts)

Bind off 1 st at armhole edge of next 4 rows. (28, 31, 31, 33 sts)

Work even until armhole measures 6½ (7¼, 7¾, 8) inches, ending with a WS row.

Shape front neck & shoulder

Next row (RS): Bind off 3 sts at beg of next row, pat to end. (25, 28, 28, 30 sts)

Dec 1 st at neck edge [every row] 5 (6, 6, 6) times, then [every other row] row 6 times. (14, 16, 16, 18 sts)

At the same time, when armhole measures 6½ (7¼, 7¾, 8) inches, bind off 4 (5, 5, 6) sts at shoulder edge once, then 5 (5, 5, 6) sts once, and 5 (6, 6, 6) sts once.

Sleeves

With size 5 needles and C, cast on 41 (43, 47, 49) sts.

Work ribbing as for back, inc 1 st on last row. (42, 44, 48, 50 sts)

Change to size 7 needles, and work Rows 1 and 2 of Ridged Stripes pat.

Setup row: With B, k1 (2, 1, 2), work Row 3 of Ridged Stripes pat to last 1 (2, 1, 2) sts, knit to end.

Continue in pat as established, and inc 1 st each end on Row 5 of pat, then [every 4th row] 6 times, then [every 6th row] 4 (6, 7, 7) times, then [every 8th row] 3 times, working new sts into pat. (70, 76, 82, 84 sts)

Work even until piece measures 11½ (12½, 14, 15½) inches from beg. Place markers at both ends.

Shape sleeve cap

Work even for 1 inch.

Dec 1 st each end every row 7 times. (56, 62, 68, 70 sts)

With A, bind off.

Front Edging

Sew shoulder seams.

With size 5 needles and C, pick up and knit 88 (94, 100, 106) sts along front edge of left front. Leave sts on a spare needle.

Rep on right front.

Hood

Left Side

With size 6 needles, cast on 2 sts.

Row 1 (RS): Knit.

Row 2: P1, M1, p1. (3 sts)

Row 3: K1, M1, knit to end. (4 sts)

Row 4: Purl to last st, M1, p1. (5 sts)

Continuing in St st, inc 1 st at same edge (this is back edge) on every row until there are 19 (20, 21, 21) sts on needle.

For Size 6 only: Work 1 row even.

Next row (RS): Cable cast on 13 (14, 15, 15) sts, knit to end of row. (32, 34, 36, 36 sts)

Change to size 7 needles, and work 4 rows even.

Inc 1 st at back neck edge on next row, then [every 4th row] 4 times. (37, 39, 41, 41 sts)

Work even until piece measures 7½ (7½, 8, 8) inches from cable cast-on edge.

Dec 1 st at back edge on next row, then [every other row] 6 times, then [every row] 4 times.

At the same time, when 30 sts rem, *bind off 2 sts at front edge, then dec 1 at front edge on next row, then bind off 2 sts at front edge. (21, 23, 25, 25 sts)

Bind off all sts.

Right Side

With size 6 needles, cast on 2 sts.

Row 1 (RS): Knit.

Row 2: P1, M1, p1. (3 sts)

Row 3: Knit to last st, M1, k1. (4 sts)

Row 4: P1, M1, purl to end. (5 sts)

Continuing in St st, inc 1 st at same edge (this is the back edge) on every row until there are 19 (20, 21, 21) sts on needle.

For Sizes 4 (8, 10) only: Work 1 row even.

Next row (WS): Cable cast on 13 (14, 15, 15) sts, purl to end of row. (32, 34, 36, 36 sts)

Work shaping for top as for left side.

Bind off all sts.

With RS facing, sew back hood seam.

Hood Band

With RS facing, using circular needle and A, pick up and knit 115 (117, 127, 129) sts along front edge of hood.

Next row (WS): P1, *k1, p1; rep from * to end.

Work 6 more rows in rib.

Next row: Change to C, and work rib. Leave sts on circular needle.

Finishing
Sew hood to neck, easing around neck shaping, and aligning the C stripes on fronts.

    With RS facing, slide sts from right front to circular needle holding hood; slide sts from left front edge to the other end of the circular needle.

Next row (RS): With C, bind off purlwise up front, bind off in rib across hood, then bind off purlwise down front.

Following instructions on page 159, insert zipper so that front stripe edges meet and conceal teeth.

    Sew sleeves into armholes, aligning markers on sleeve with body underarm.

    Sew side and sleeve seams.

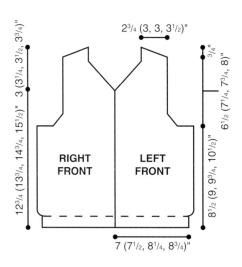

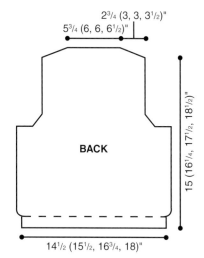

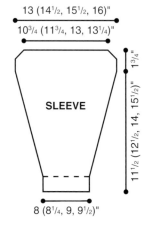

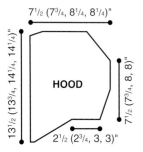

DESIGN BY MELISSA LEAPMAN

Dad's Block Stitch Crew

Sizes

INTERMEDIATE

Man's small (medium, large, extra-large) Instructions are given for smallest size, with larger sizes in parentheses. When only 1 number is given, it applies to all sizes.

Finished Measurements

Chest: 40 (45, 51, 56) inches
Length: 23½ (24, 24, 24½) inches

Materials

4 MEDIUM

• Plymouth Galway Worsted 100 percent wool (210 yds/100g per ball) medium weight yarn: 9 (10, 10, 11) balls dusty teal #738
• Size 6 (4mm) needles
• Size 8 (5mm) needles or size needed to obtain gauge
• Tapestry needle

Gauge

24 sts and 26 rows = 4 inches/ 10cm in Block St pat with larger needles,
To save time, take time to check gauge.

Pattern Stitches

A. K2 P2 Rib (multiple of 4 sts)
Row 1: *K2, p2; rep from * across.
Rep Row 1 for pat.
B. Block Stitch
See Chart on page 76.

Back

With smaller needles, cast on 120 (136, 152, 168) sts.
   Beg K2 P2 Rib, and work even until piece measures approx 3 inches from beg, ending with a WS row.

Change to larger needles, and beg Block St pat where indicated on Chart.
   Work even until piece measures approx 13½ inches from beg, ending with a WS row.

Shape Armholes

Bind off 12 (12, 16, 20) sts at beg of next 2 rows. (96, 112, 120, 128 sts)

Work even until armhole measures approx 9½ (10, 10, 10½) inches, ending with a WS row.

Shape Shoulders

Bind off 8 (11, 12, 13) sts at beg of next 4 rows, then bind off 8 (10, 12, 14) sts at beg of next 2 rows. (48 sts)
   Bind off rem sts for back of neck.

Dad and son will both look great in their blocks-in-blocks pullovers.

Front

Work as for back until armhole measures approx 7½ (8, 8, 8½) inches, ending with a WS row.

Shape Neck

Continuing pat as established, work across first 39 (47, 51, 55) sts, join 2nd ball of yarn and bind off the center 8 sts, work across to end row.

Work both sides at once with separate balls of yarn, and bind off at each neck edge [4 sts] twice, then [2 sts] once, then dec 1 st at each neck edge [every row] 5 times. (24, 32, 36, 40 sts rem each shoulder)

Work even until armhole measures same as back to shoulder.

Shape shoulders as for back.

Sleeves

With smaller needles, cast on 60 sts.

Beg K2 P2 Rib, and work even until piece measures approx 3 inches from beg, ending with a WS row.

Change to larger needles, and beg Block St pat where indicated on Chart.

Inc 1 st each side [every other row] 2 (12, 13, 21) times, then [every 4th row] 25 (18, 17, 12) times. (114, 120, 120, 126 sts)

Work even until piece measures approx 22 (21, 21, 21½) inches from beg.

Bind off.

Neck Band

Sew right shoulder seam.

With RS facing and smaller needles, pick up and knit 112 sts.

Work K2 P2 Rib pat until band measures approx 1 inch from beg.

Bind off loosely in pat.

Assembly

Sew left shoulder seam, including side of neck band.

Sew sleeves into armholes.

Sew side and sleeve seams. ✐

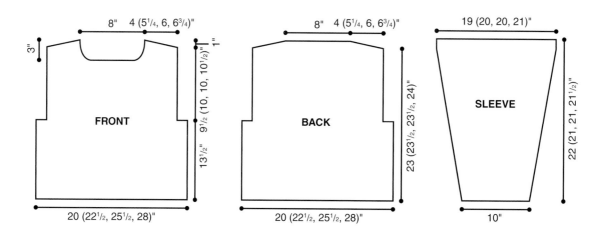

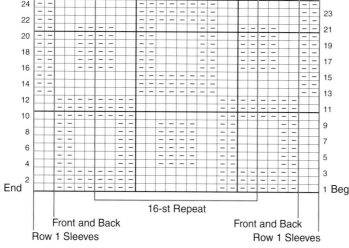

BLOCK STITCH CHART

16-st Repeat

Front and Back Row 1 Sleeves

Front and Back Row 1 Sleeves

End · Beg

STITCH KEY
- ⊟ K on RS; p on WS
- ☐ P on RS; k on WS

DESIGN BY MELISSA LEAPMAN

Son's Block Stitch Crew

Sizes

INTERMEDIATE

Child's 8 (10, 12, 14) Instructions are given for smallest size, with larger sizes in parentheses. When only 1 number is given, it applies to all sizes.

Finished Measurements

Chest: 32 (34½, 37, 40) inches
Length: 14 (15½, 16½, 17) inches

Materials

4 MEDIUM

• Plymouth Galway Worsted 100 percent wool (210 yds/100g per ball) medium weight yarn: 5 (5, 6, 7) balls mustard #744
• Size 6 (4mm) needles
• Size 8 (5mm) needles or size needed to obtain gauge
• Tapestry needle

Gauge

24 sts and 26 rows = 4 inches/ 10cm in Block St pat with larger needles
To save time, take time to check gauge.

Pattern Stitches

A. K2 P2 Rib (multiple of 4 sts)
Row 1: *K2, p2; rep from * across. Rep Row 1 for pat.
B. Block Stitch
See Chart on page 79.

Back

With smaller needles, cast on 96 (104, 112, 120) sts.
   Beg K2 P2 Rib, and work even until piece measures approx 2 inches from beg, ending with a WS row.

   Change to larger needles, and beg Block St pat where indicated on Chart.
   Work even until piece measures approx 7¼ (8½, 9¼, 9½) inches from beg, ending with a WS row.

Shape Armholes

Bind off 8 (8, 12, 12) sts at beg of next 2 rows. (80, 88, 88, 96 sts)
   Work even until armhole measures approx 6¾ (7, 7¼, 7½) inches, ending with a WS row.

Shape Shoulders

Bind off 8 (9, 9, 9) sts at beg of next 4 rows, then bind off 8 (8, 8, 10) sts at beg of next 4 rows. (32, 36, 36, 40 sts)
   Bind off rem sts for back of neck.

Front

Work as for back until armhole measures approx 5¾ (6, 6¼, 6½) inches, ending with a WS row.

Shape Neck

Continuing pat as established, work 33 (36, 36, 38) sts, join 2nd ball of

This complicated-
looking stitch is
just knits and
purls. Go for it!

yarn and bind off center 14 (16, 16, 20) sts, work to end row.

Working both sides at once with separate balls of yarn, bind off at each neck edge [4 (5, 5, 5) sts] once, then [3 sts] once, then dec 1 st at each neck edge [every row] twice. (24, 26, 26, 28 sts rem each shoulder)

Work even until piece measures same as back to shoulder.

Shape shoulders as for back.

Sleeves

With smaller needles, cast on 48 (48, 52, 52) sts

Beg K2 P2 Rib, and work even until piece measures approx 2 inches from beg, ending with a WS row.

Change to larger needles, and beg Block St pat where indicated on Chart.

Inc 1 st each side [every 4th row] 17 (15, 10, 11) times, then [every 6th row] 0 (3, 8, 8) times. (82, 84, 88, 90 sts)

Work even until piece measures approx 15¼ (16½, 18½, 19) inches from beg.

Bind off.

Neck Band

Sew right shoulder seam.

With RS facing and smaller needles, pick up and knit 72 (76, 76, 80) sts.

Work K2 P2 Rib until band measures approx 1 inch from beg.

Bind off loosely in pat.

Assembly

Sew left shoulder seam, including side of neck band.

Sew sleeves into armholes.

Sew side and sleeve seams. ❧

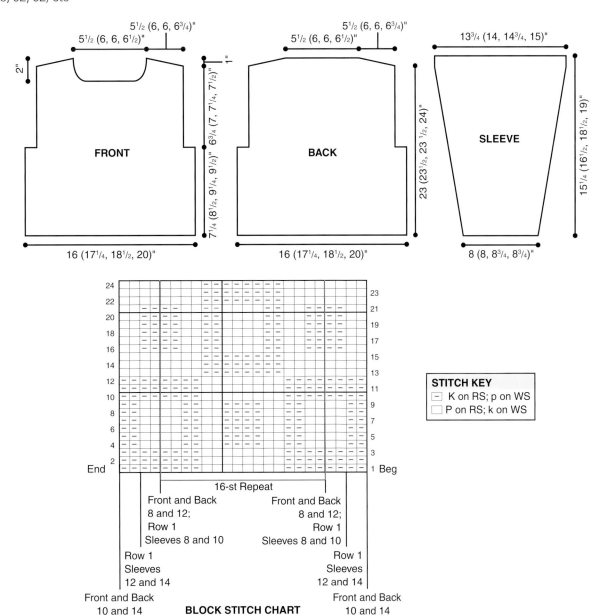

FRONT

BACK

SLEEVE

5½ (6, 6, 6¾)"

5½ (6, 6, 6½)"

2"

1"

6¾ (7, 7¼, 7½)"

7¼ (8½, 9¼, 9½)"

16 (17¼, 18½, 20)"

5½ (6, 6, 6¾)"

5½ (6, 6, 6½)"

23 (23½, 23 ½, 24)"

16 (17¼, 18½, 20)"

13¾ (14, 14¾, 15)"

15¼ (16½, 18½, 19)"

8 (8, 8¾, 8¾)"

STITCH KEY
⊟ K on RS; p on WS
☐ P on RS; k on WS

16-st Repeat

Front and Back
8 and 12;
Row 1
Sleeves 8 and 10

Front and Back
8 and 12;
Row 1
Sleeves 8 and 10

Row 1
Sleeves
12 and 14

Row 1
Sleeves
12 and 14

Front and Back
10 and 14

Front and Back
10 and 14

End

Beg

BLOCK STITCH CHART

DESIGN BY CELESTE PINHEIRO

Alpine Family Men's Pullover

Sizes

EXPERIENCED

Men's small (medium, large, extra-large) Instructions are given for smallest size, with larger sizes in parentheses. When only 1 number is given, it applies to all sizes.

Finished Measurements

Chest: 40 (44, 48, 52) inches
Length: 24 (25, 26, 27) inches

Materials

4 MEDIUM

- Plymouth Encore Worsted 75 percent acrylic/25 percent wool medium weight yarn (200yds/100g per ball): 5 (6, 6, 7) balls dark gray #520 (MC); 1 ball each natural #146 (A), red #1386 (B), blue #4045 (C), light gray #194 (D) and tan #4379 (E)
- Size 6 (4mm) needles
- Size 8 (5mm) needles or size needed to obtain gauge
- Size 9 (5.5mm) needles or size needed to obtain gauge
- Tapestry needle

Gauge

18 sts and 19 rows = 4 inches/ 10cm in Fair Isle pat with size 9 needles
18 sts and 25 rows = 4 inches/ 10cm in Pebble Rib pat with size 8 needles
To save time, take time to check gauge.

Family members will enjoy wearing these sweaters during the holidays and all winter long.

Pattern Stitches

A. Braid (multiple of 2 sts + 1)
Row 1 (WS): *P1 MC, p1 A; rep from * to last st, p1 MC.
Row 2: Carrying both yarns in front and bringing one strand over the previous strand when working it, *p1 MC, p1 A; rep from * to last st, p1 MC. The floats will be on the RS, and will spiral to the right. *Do not untwist ends.*
Row 3: Carrying both yarns in back and bringing one strand over the previous strand when working it, *k1 MC, k1 A; rep from * to last st, k1 MC. The floats will be on the RS, and will spiral to the left. The yarn ends will untwist as you work this row.
B. Fair Isle pattern (12 st rep)
See Chart (Rows 1–43).
C. Pebble Rib (multiple of 3 sts)
See Chart (Rows 44–45).

Back

With size 6 needles and MC, cast on 91 (97, 109, 115) sts.
Purl 11 rows, ending with a RS row.
Next 3 rows: Change to size 8 needles and work Braid pat.
Next row (WS): Change to size 9 needles and beg Fair Isle pat where indicated on the Chart.
Work Rows 1–10 of Fair Isle pat.
Change to size 8 needles and beg Pebble Rib where indicated on the Chart.
Work even in Pebble Rib as established until piece measures 12½ (13½, 14½, 15½) inches from beg, ending with a RS row.
Change to size 9 needles and work Rows 1–43 of Fair Isle pat, beg where indicated on the Chart.
Work even until piece measures 15 (15½, 16½, 17) inches from beg, ending with a WS row.

Shape armholes

Dec 1 st each side on next row, then [every other row] 5 times more. (79, 85, 97, 103 sts)
When Fair Isle pat is complete, change to size 8 needles and work in Pebble Rib until armhole measures 8½ (9, 9, 9½) inches, ending with a WS row.

Shape back neck

Continuing pat as established, work 20 (23, 28, 31) sts, join 2nd ball of yarn and bind off center 39 (39, 41, 41) sts, work to end of row.
Next row: Working both sides at once with separate balls of yarn, dec 1 st at each neck edge. (19, 22, 27, 30 sts rem each shoulder)
Work even until armhole measures 9 (9½, 9½, 10) inches.
Bind off.

Front

Work as for back until armhole measures 6½ (7, 7, 7½) inches, ending with a WS row. **Note:** *Fair Isle pat should be complete.*

Shape front neck

Continuing pat as established, work 32 (35, 41, 43) sts, join 2nd ball of yarn and bind off center 15 (15, 17, 17) sts, work to end of row.
Working both sides at once with separate balls of yarn, at each neck edge bind off [4 sts] once, [3 sts] twice, [2 sts] once, [1 st] once. (19, 22, 27, 30 sts rem each shoulder)
Work even until armhole measures 9 (9½, 9½, 10) inches.
Bind off.

Sleeve

With smaller needles and MC, cast on 43 (43, 47, 47) sts.
Knit 11 rows, ending with a WS row.

Next 3 rows: Change to size 8 needles and work Braid pat.
Next row (WS): Change to size 9 needles and beg Fair Isle pat where indicated on Chart.
Work Rows 1–10 of Fair Isle pat, and *at the same time*, inc 1 st each side on Row 4 of pat, then [every 4 rows] 18 (20, 18, 20) times, working new sts in pat. (81, 85, 85, 89 sts)
Change to size 8 needles and beg Pebble Rib where indicated on Chart.
Continue in Pebble Rib and complete inc.
Work even until sleeve measures 21 (21, 22, 22) inches from beg, or desired length, ending with a WS row.

Shape sleeve cap

Dec 1 st each side on next row, then [every other row] 5 times more. (69, 73, 73, 77 sts)
Bind off.

Neck Band

Sew right shoulder seam.
With RS facing and using size 6 needles and MC, pick up and knit 103 (103, 107, 107) sts evenly around neck.
Next row (WS): Knit.
Next 3 rows: Change to size 8 needles and work Braid pat.
Next 6 rows: Change to size 6 needles, and with MC, purl.
Bind off purlwise.

Assembly

Sew left shoulder seam, including side of neck band.
Sew sleeves into armholes.
Sew side and sleeve seams.

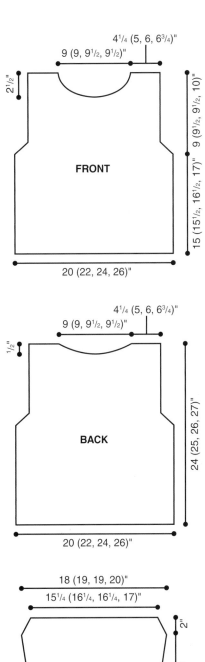

4¼ (5, 6, 6¾)"

9 (9, 9½, 9½)"

2½"

FRONT

15 (15½, 16½, 17)" 9 (9½, 9½, 10)"

20 (22, 24, 26)"

4¼ (5, 6, 6¾)"

9 (9, 9½, 9½)"

½"

BACK

24 (25, 26, 27)"

20 (22, 24, 26)"

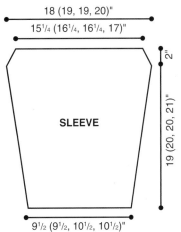

18 (19, 19, 20)"

15¼ (16¼, 16¼, 17)"

2"

SLEEVE

19 (20, 20, 21)"

9½ (9½, 10½, 10½)"

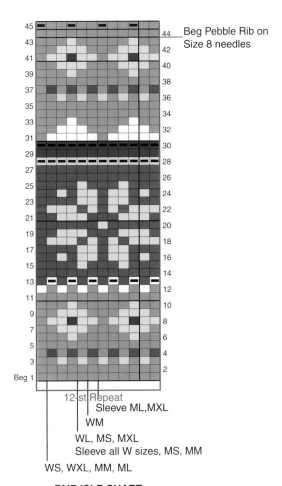

Beg Pebble Rib on
Size 8 needles

12-st Repeat
Sleeve ML, MXL
WM
WL, MS, MXL
Sleeve all W sizes, MS, MM
WS, WXL, MM, ML

FAIR ISLE CHART
(Men's and Women's)

COLOR KEY
- Dark gray (MC)
- Natural (A)
- Red (B)
- Blue (C)
- Light gray (D)
- Tan (E)
- K on RS, p on WS

DESIGN BY CELESTE PINHEIRO

Alpine Family Women's Pullover

Sizes

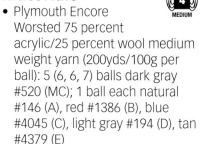
EXPERIENCED

Woman's small (medium, large, extra-large) Instructions are given for smallest size, with larger sizes in parentheses. When only 1 number is given, it applies to all sizes.

Finished Measurements

Chest: 38 (41½, 46, 48½) inches
Length: 20 (22, 23, 25) inches (excluding fringe)

Materials

4 MEDIUM

- Plymouth Encore Worsted 75 percent acrylic/25 percent wool medium weight yarn (200yds/100g per ball): 5 (6, 6, 7) balls dark gray #520 (MC); 1 ball each natural #146 (A), red #1386 (B), blue #4045 (C), light gray #194 (D), tan #4379 (E)
- Size 6 (4mm) needles
- Size 8 (5mm) needles or size needed to obtain gauge
- Size 9 (5.5mm) needles or size needed to obtain gauge
- Size G/6 (4mm) crochet hook for attaching fringe
- Tapestry needle

Gauge

18 sts and 19 rows = 4 inches/ 10cm in Fair Isle pat with size 9 needles
18 sts and 25 rows = 4 inches/ 10cm in Pebble Rib pat with size 8 needles

To save time, take time to check gauge.

Pattern Stitches

A. Braid (multiple of 2 sts + 1)
Row 1 (WS): *P1 MC, p1 A; rep from * to last st, p1 MC.
Row 2: Carrying both yarns in front and bringing one strand over the previous strand when working it, *p1 MC, p1 A; rep from * to last st, p1 MC. The floats will be on the RS, and will spiral to the right. *Do not untwist ends.*
Row 3: Carrying both yarns in back and bringing one strand over the previous strand when working it, *k1 MC, k1 A; rep from * to last st, k1 MC. The floats will be on the RS, and will spiral to the left. The yarn ends will untwist as you work this row.
B. Fair Isle pattern (12-st rep)
See Chart on page 83 (Rows 1–43).
C. Pebble Rib (multiple of 3 sts)
See Chart on page 83 (Rows 44 and 45).

Back

With size 6 needles and MC, cast on 85 (93, 103, 109) sts.
Knit 11 rows.
Next 3 rows: Change to size 8 needles, and work Braid pat.
Next row (WS): Change to size 9 needles, and beg Fair Isle pat where indicated on Chart.
Work Rows 1–43 of Fair Isle pat.
Change to size 8 needles, and beg Pebble Rib where indicated on Chart.

Work even in Pebble Rib as established until piece measures 11½ (13, 14, 14½) inches from beg, ending with a WS row.

Shape armhole

Bind off 5 sts at beg of next 2 rows. (75, 83, 93, 99 sts)
Dec 1 st each side on next row, then [every other row] 3 times more. (67, 75, 85, 91 sts)
Work even in Pebble Rib until armhole measures 8 (8½, 8½, 9) inches, ending with a WS row.

Shape back neck

Continuing pat as established, work 19 (22, 26, 27) sts, join 2nd ball of yarn and bind off center 29 (31, 33, 37) sts, work to end of row.
Next row: Working both sides at once with separate balls of yarn, dec 1 st at each neck edge. (18, 21, 25, 26 sts rem each shoulder)
Work even until armhole measures 8½ (9, 9, 9½) inches.
Bind off.

Front

Work as for back until armhole measures 6¾ (7¼, 7¼, 8¼) inches, ending with a WS row.

Front neck shaping

Continuing pat as established, work 28 (32, 36, 39) sts, join 2nd ball of yarn and bind off center 11 (11, 13, 15) sts, work to end of row.
Working both sides at once with

A fringe trim at the bottom of this sweater adds a feminine touch for Mom.

separate balls of yarn, at each neck edge bind off [4 sts] once, [3 sts] once, [2 sts] 1 (1, 1, 2) times, [1 st] 1 (2, 2, 1) times. (18, 21, 25, 26 sts rem each shoulder)

Work even until armhole measures 8½ (9, 9, 9½) inches.

Bind off.

Sleeve

With size 6 needles and MC, cast on 43 sts.

Knit 17 rows, ending with a WS row.

Next 3 rows: Change to size 8 needles and work Braid pat.

Next row (WS): Change to size 9 needles and beg Fair Isle pat where indicated on the Chart.

Work Rows 1–10 of Fair Isle pat and *at the same time*, inc 1 st each side on Row 4 of pat, then [every 4 rows] 6 (12, 12, 17) times, then

[every 6 rows] 10 (6, 6, 3) times, working new sts in pat. (77, 81, 81, 85 sts)

Change to size 8 needles and beg Pebble Rib where indicated on Chart.

Cont in Pebble Rib and complete inc.

Work even until sleeve measures 20 (19, 18, 18) inches from beg, or desired length, ending with a WS row.

Shape sleeve cap

Dec 1 st each side on next row, then [every other row] 3 times more. (69, 73, 73, 77 sts)

Bind off.

Neck Band

Sew right shoulder seam.

With RS facing and using size 6 needles and MC, pick up and knit

77 (81, 85, 89) sts around neck.

Next row (WS): Knit.

Next 3 rows: Change to size 8 needles, and work Braid pat.

Next 5 rows: Change to size 6 needles, and with MC, purl.

Bind off purlwise.

Assembly

Sew left shoulder seam, including side of neck band.

Sew sleeves into armholes.

Sew side and sleeve seams.

Fringe

Following instructions on page 161, attach fringe as follows: Cut 170 (186, 206, 218) 6-inch strands of MC for fringe. Using crochet hook, attach 2 strands-per-fringe in every other st along bottom edge.

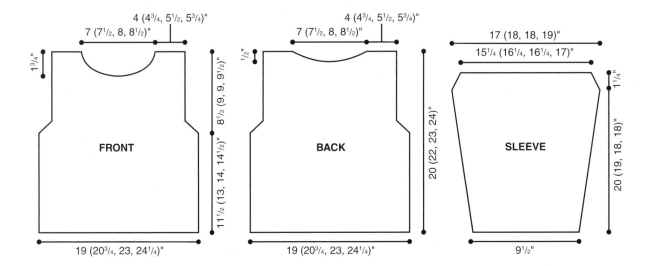

DESIGN BY CELESTE PINHEIRO

Alpine Family Boy's Vest

Sizes

EXPERIENCED

Child's 4 (6, 8, 10, 12) Instructions are given for smallest size, with larger sizes in parentheses. When only 1 number is given, it applies to all sizes.

Finished Measurements

Chest: 25½ (27, 30, 32½, 35) inches
Length: 14 (15, 16, 17, 18) inches

Materials

- Plymouth Encore Worsted 75 percent acrylic/25 percent wool, (200yds/100g per ball) medium weight yarn: 2 (2, 2, 3, 3) balls red #1386 (MC); 1 ball each dark gray #520 (A), natural #146 (B), blue #4045 (C), light gray #194 (D), tan #4379 (E) **4 MEDIUM**
- Size 6 (4mm) straight and 16-inch circular needles
- Size 8 (5mm) needles or size needed to obtain gauge
- Size 9 (5.5mm) needles or size needed to obtain gauge
- Tapestry needle

Gauge

18 sts and 19 rows = 4 inches/ 10cm in Fair Isle pat with size 9 needles
18 sts and 25 rows = 4 inches/ 10cm in Pebble Rib pat with size 8 needles
To save time, take time to check gauge.

Pattern Stitches

A. Braid (multiple of 2 sts + 1)
Row 1 (RS): *K1 A, k1 B; rep from * to last st, k1 A.

Row 2: Carrying both yarns in back and bringing one strand over the previous strand when working it, *k1 A, k1 B; rep from * to last st, k1 A. The floats will be on the RS, and will spiral to the right. *Do not untwist ends.*

Row 3: Carrying both yarns in front and bringing one strand over the previous strand when working it, *p1 A, p1 B; rep from * to last st, p1 A. The floats will be on the RS, and will spiral to the left. The yarn ends will untwist as you work this row.

B. Fair Isle pattern (12-st rep)
See Chart on page 89 (Rows 1–43).
C. Pebble Rib (multiple of 3 sts)
See Chart on page 89 (Rows 44 and 45).

Pattern Note

On smaller sizes, the shaping will begin before Fair Isle pat is complete. Work in pat while shaping.

Back

With smaller needles and MC, cast on 57 (61, 67, 73, 79) sts.
Knit 9 rows, ending with a WS row.
Next 3 rows: Change to size 8 needles and work Braid pat.
Next row (WS): Change to size 9 needles, and beg Fair Isle pat where indicated on Chart.

Work Rows 1–43 of Fair Isle pat (see Pattern Note).
Change to size 8 needles, and beg Pebble Rib where indicated on Chart.
Work even in Pebble Rib as established until piece measures 9 (9½, 10, 10½, 11) inches from beg, ending with a WS row.

Shape armholes

Dec 1 st each side on next row, then [every other row] 4 times more. (47, 51, 57, 63, 69 sts)
Work even until armhole measures 4½ (5, 5½, 6, 6½) inches, ending with a WS row.

Shape back neck

Continuing pat as established, work 12 (14, 16, 19, 21) sts, join

What a great little vest for those dress-up occasions!

2nd ball of yarn and bind off center 23 (23, 25, 25, 27) sts, work to end of row.

Next row: Working both sides at once with separate balls of yarn, dec 1 st at each neck edge. (11, 13, 15, 18, 20 rem each shoulder)

Work even until armhole measures 5 (5½, 6, 6½, 7) inches.

Bind off.

Front

Work as for back until armhole measures 1 (1½, 2, 2, 2) inches, ending with a WS row.

Shape V-neck

Continuing pat as established,

work 23 (25, 28, 31, 34) sts, join 2nd ball of yarn, k2tog, work to end of row.

Working both sides at once with separate balls of yarn, work 1 row even in pat as established.

Dec row: Work to 3 sts before neck edge, ssk, k1; k1, k2tog, work to end of row.

Rep Dec row [every other row] 11 (11, 12, 12, 13) times more. (11, 13, 15, 18, 20 sts rem each shoulder)

Work even until armhole measures 5 (5½, 6, 6½, 7) inches.

Bind off.

Neck Band

Sew shoulder seams.

With RS facing, using circular needle and MC, pick up and knit 78 (82, 86, 86, 90) sts evenly around neck. Do not join.

Knit 3 rows.

Bind off knitwise.

Armhole Edge

With smaller needles and MC pick up 56 (60, 66, 70, 76) sts evenly around armhole.

Work as for neck band.

Assembly

Sew side seams.

Tack down front overlap of neck edging.

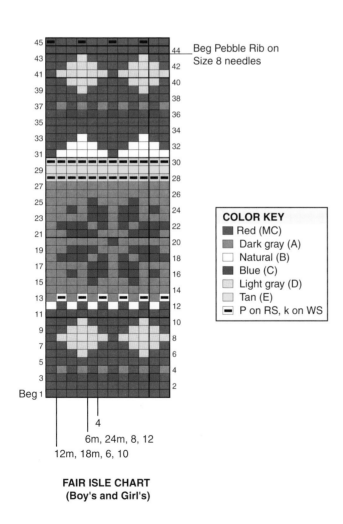

COLOR KEY
- Red (MC)
- Dark gray (A)
- Natural (B)
- Blue (C)
- Light gray (D)
- Tan (E)
- P on RS, k on WS

Beg Pebble Rib on Size 8 needles

4

6m, 24m, 8, 12

12m, 18m, 6, 10

FAIR ISLE CHART
(Boy's and Girl's)

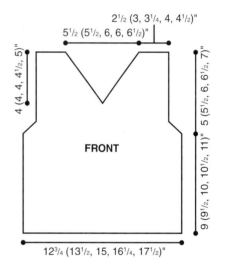

FRONT

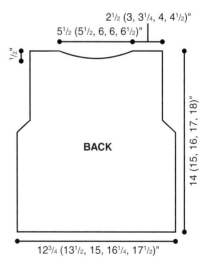

BACK

Alpine Family Girl's Pullover

DESIGN BY CELESTE PINHEIRO

Sizes

Child's 4 (6, 8, 10, 12) Instructions are given for smallest size, with larger sizes in parentheses. When only 1 number is given, it applies to all sizes.

Finished Measurements

Chest: 25½ (27, 30, 32½, 35) inches
Length: 14 (15, 16, 17, 18) inches

Materials

- Plymouth Encore Worsted 75 percent acrylic/25 percent wool medium weight yarn (200yds/100g per ball): 2 (2, 2, 3, 3) balls red #1386 (MC); 1 ball each dark gray #520 (A), natural #146 (B), blue #4045 (C), light gray #194 (D), tan #4379 (E)
- Size 6 (4mm) needles
- Size 8 (5mm) needles or size needed to obtain gauge
- Size 9 (5.5mm) needles or size needed to obtain gauge
- Size G/6 (4mm) crochet hook for attaching fringe
- Tapestry needle

Gauge

18 sts and 19 rows = 4 inches/ 10cm in Fair Isle pat with size 9 needles
18 sts and 25 rows = 4 inches/ 10cm in Pebble Rib pat with size 8 needles
To save time, take time to check gauge.

Pattern Stitches

A. Braid (multiple of 2 sts + 1)
Row 1 (RS): *K1 A, k1 B; rep from * to last st, k1 A.
Row 2: Carrying both yarns in back and bringing one strand over the previous strand when working it, *k1 A, k1 B; rep from * to last st, k1 A. The floats will be on the RS, and will spiral to the right. *Do not untwist ends.*
Row 3: Carrying both yarns in front and bringing one strand over the previous strand when working it, *p1 A, p1 B; rep from * to last st, p1 A. The floats will be on the RS, and will spiral to the left. The yarn ends will untwist as you work this row.
B. Fair Isle pattern (12-st rep)
See Chart on page 89 (Rows 1–43).
C. Pebble Rib (multiple of 3 sts)
See Chart on page 89 (Rows 44 and 45).

Back

With smaller needles and MC, cast on 57 (61, 67, 73, 79) sts.
Knit 9 rows, ending with a WS row.
Next 3 rows: Change to size 8 needles and work Braid pat.
Next row (WS): Change to size 9 needles and beg Fair Isle pat where indicated on the Chart.
Work Rows 1–43 of Fair Isle pat.
Change to size 8 needles, and beg Pebble Rib where indicated on Chart.
Continue in Pebble Rib as established until piece measures 13½ (14½, 15½, 16½, 17½) inches from beg, ending with a WS row.

Shape back neck

Continuing pat as established, work 17 (19, 21, 24, 26) sts, join 2nd ball of yarn and bind off center 23 (23, 25, 25, 27) sts, work to end of row.
Next row: Working both sides at once with separate balls of yarn, dec 1 st at each neck edge. (16, 18, 20, 23, 25 sts rem each shoulder)
Work even until piece measures 14 (15, 16, 17, 18) inches from beg.
Bind off.

Front

Work as for back until piece measures 12 (13, 14, 15, 16) inches from beg, ending with a WS row.

Shape front neck

Continuing pat as established, work 24 (26, 29, 32, 34) sts, join 2nd ball of yarn and bind off center 9 (9, 9, 9, 11) sts, work to end of row.
Working both sides at once with separate balls of yarn, at each neck edge bind off [3 sts] once, [2 sts] twice, [1 st] 1 (1, 2, 2, 2) times. (16, 18, 20, 23, 25 sts rem each shoulder)
Work even until piece measures 14 (15, 16, 17, 18) inches.
Bind off.

Sleeve

With smaller needles and MC, cast on 33 (33, 35, 37, 37) sts.

Edged with braid and fringe, this colorful sweater is sure to be any girl's favorite.

Knit 5 rows, ending with a WS row.
Next 3 rows: Change to size 8 needles, and work Braid pat.
Next row: Purl.
Setup row (RS): Change to MC and beg Pebble Rib as follows: K2 (2, 2, 1, 1), *p1, k2; rep from * to last 1 (1, 0, 0, 0) st(s), end k1 (1, 0, 0, 0).

Continue in Pebble Rib as established and *at the same time*, inc 1 st each side [every 4 rows] 10 (11, 12, 12, 13) times, working new sts in pat. (53, 55, 59, 61, 63 sts)

Work even until piece measures 10 (11, 12, 13, 14) inches from beg, or desired length, ending with a WS row.

Bind off.

Neck Band

Sew right shoulder seam.
With RS facing and using size 6 needles and MC, pick up and knit 57 (57, 61, 61, 65) sts evenly around neck.
Next row (WS): Knit.
Next 3 rows: Change to size 8 needles and A and B. Work Braid pat.

Change to size 6 needles and C, and work in St st until band measures 2½ inches from pickup row.

Bind off loosely.

Assembly

Sew left shoulder and neck band.
Place markers on front and back, 6 (6¼, 6½, 6¾, 7) inches from shoulder. Sew sleeves between markers.

Sew side and sleeve seams.

Fringe

Following instructions on page 161, attach fringe as follows: Cut 114 (122, 134, 146, 158) 5-inch strands of MC for fringe. Use crochet hook to attach 2 strands-per-fringe in every other st along bottom edge.

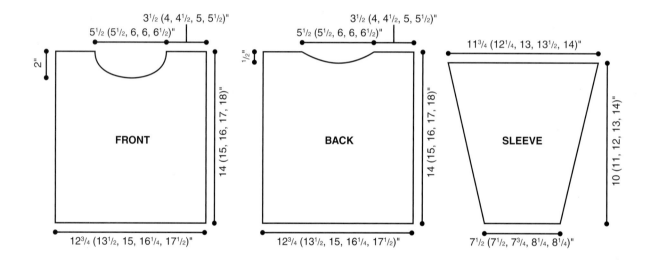

Alpine Family Baby Hoodie

DESIGN BY CELESTE PINHEIRO

Sizes

Infant's 6 (12, 18, 24) months Instructions are given for smallest size, with larger sizes in parentheses. When only 1 number is given, it applies to all sizes.

EXPERIENCED

Finished Measurements

Chest: 20 (22, 24, 26) inches
Length: 10 (11, 12, 13)

Materials

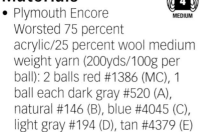

- Plymouth Encore Worsted 75 percent acrylic/25 percent wool medium weight yarn (200yds/100g per ball): 2 balls red #1386 (MC), 1 ball each dark gray #520 (A), natural #146 (B), blue #4045 (C), light gray #194 (D), tan #4379 (E)
- Size 6 (4mm) needles and 29-inch circular needle
- Size 8 (5mm) needles or size needed to obtain gauge
- Size 9 (5.5mm) needles or size needed to obtain gauge
- Stitch holders
- Tapestry needle
- Cardboard, 4½ inches wide
- 6 [⅝-inch] buttons

Gauge

18 sts and 19 rows = 4 inches/10cm in Fair Isle pat with size 9 needles
18 sts and 25 rows = 4 inches/10cm in Pebble Rib pat with size 8 needles
To save time, take time to check gauge.

Pattern Stitches

A. Braid (multiple of 2 sts + 1)

Row 1 (RS): *K1 A, k1 B; rep from * to last st, k1 A.

Row 2: Carrying both yarns in back and bringing one strand over the previous strand when working it, *k1 A, k1 B; rep from * to last st, k1 A. The floats will be on the RS, and will spiral to the right. *Do not untwist ends.*

Row 3: Carrying both yarns in front and bringing one strand over the previous strand when working it, *p1 A, p1 B; rep from * to last st, p1. The floats will be on the RS, and will spiral to the left. The yarn ends will untwist as you work this row.

B. Fair Isle pattern (12-st rep)
See Chart A on page 89 (Rows 1–43).

C. Pebble Rib (multiple of 3 sts)
See Fair Isle Chart on page 89 (Rows 44 and 45).

D. Stripe pattern
See Chart B on page 95.

Pattern Notes

On smaller sizes, the shaping will begin before Fair Isle pat is complete. Work in pat while shaping.

Body is worked in one piece, then divided for front and back.

Body

With smaller needles and MC, cast on 91 (97, 109, 115) sts.

Knit 7 rows, ending with a WS row.

Next 3 rows: Change to size 8 needles, and work Braid pat.

Next row (WS): Change to size 9 needles and beg Fair Isle pat where indicated on Chart A.

Work even until piece measures 6 (6½, 7, 7½) inches from beg, ending with a WS row.

Divide for fronts and back

Work 23 (24, 27, 29) sts and place on holder for left front; work 45 (49, 55, 59) sts for back; place rem 23 (24, 27, 29) sts on holder for right front.

Back

When Fair Isle pat is complete, change to size 8 needles and work Pebble Rib, beg where indicated on Chart A.

Work even until back measures

This cozy hoodie is sized to bundle up babies from 6 to 24 months.

9½ (10½, 11½, 12½) inches from division, ending with a WS row.

Shape back neck
Work 12 (14, 16, 18) sts, bind off 21 (21, 23, 23) sts, work to end.
   Dec 1 st at each neck edge once. (11, 13, 15, 17 sts)
   Work even until back measures 10 (11, 12, 13) inches from division. Bind off.

Left Front
Slip sts for left front from st holder to needles.
   Work as for back until front measures 8 (10, 11, 12) inches from division, ending with a WS row.

Shape front neck
At neck edge, bind off [4 sts] once, [3 sts] once, [2 sts] 1 (1, 2, 2) times, [1 st] 2 times. (11, 13, 15, 17 sts)
   Work even until front measures 10 (11, 12, 13) inches from division. Bind off.

Right Front
Slip sts for right front from st holder to needles.
   Work as for back until front measures 8 (10, 11, 12) inches from division, ending with a RS row.

Shape front neck
At neck edge, bind off [4 sts] once, [3 sts] once, [2 sts] 1 (1, 2, 2) times, [1 st] 2 times. (11, 13, 15, 17 sts)
   Work even until front measures

10 (11, 12, 13) inches from division. Bind off.

Sleeve
With smaller needles and MC, cast on 32 (32, 36, 36) sts.
   Knit 7 rows, ending with a WS row.
Next 3 rows: Change to size 8 needles, and work Braid pat.
   Begin Stripe pat (Chart B), and *at the same time*, inc 1 st each side every [8 (8, 8, 6) rows] 2 (5, 5, 7) times. (36, 42, 46, 50 sts)
   Work even until sleeve measures 8 (9, 10, 11) inches from beg, ending with a WS row.
   Bind off.

Hood
Sew shoulder seams.
   With size 8 needles and MC, pick up and knit 45 (45, 49, 49) sts around neck.
   Work Stripe pat (Chart B) until piece measures 8 (8, 9, 9) inches from pickup, ending with a WS row.

Hood shaping
Row 1 (RS): Continuing Stripe pat as established, work 21 (21, 23, 23) sts, sk2p, work to end. (43, 43, 47, 47 sts)
Row 2 and all WS rows: Work even.
Row 3: Work 20 (20, 22, 22) sts, sk2p, work to end. (41, 41, 45, 45 sts)
Row 5: Work 19 (19, 21, 21) sts, sk2p, work to end. (39, 39, 43, 43 sts)
Row 7: Work 18 (18, 20, 20) sts,

sk2p, work to end. (37, 37, 41, 41 sts)
Row 9: Work 17 (17, 19, 19) sts, sk2p, work to end. (35, 35, 39, 39 sts)
   Bind off.

Assembly
Sew sleeves into armholes.
   Sew sleeve seams.

Buttonband
With RS facing, using circular needle and MC, pick up and knit 178 (188, 196, 204) sts evenly around right front, hood, and left front.
   Knit 3 rows, ending with a WS row.
Buttonhole row: K3, *k2tog, yo, k5 (6, 7, 8); rep from * 4 more times, k2tog, yo, knit to end.
   Knit 3 rows.
   Bind off.

Finishing
Sew buttons opposite buttonholes.
Tassel: Holding all colors tog, wind 5 times around a piece of cardboard 4½ inches wide. Cut a strand of MC approx 10 inches long, and fold in half. Pull resulting loop through loops at one end of cardboard, bring tails through the loop, and pull tight. Cut the loops at the other end of the cardboard. Cut another strand of MC approx 5 inches long and wrap the tassel below the top, gathering all strands together. Trim ends neatly. Attach to top of hood. ✌

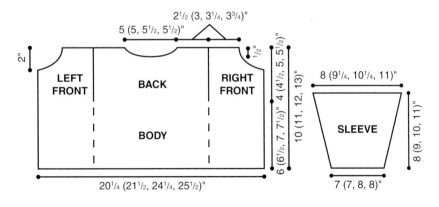

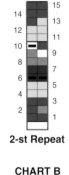

CHART B

COLOR KEY
- ■ Red (MC)
- ■ Dark gray (A)
- □ Natural (B)
- ■ Blue (C)
- ▨ Light gray (D)
- ▨ Tan (E)
- ⊟ P on RS, k on WS

2-st Repeat

HOUSE BECOMES HOME

Whether you're fixing up a new house, updating a home or making a gift, you'll find ideas here. We've included afghans, a placemat, a rug and pillow duo, and a tea cozy and hot pad set.

DESIGN BY LAURA POLLEY

Seaside At Sunset Afghan

Finished Size
Approx 45 x 54 inches

INTERMEDIATE

Materials
- Plymouth Handpaint Wool 100 percent wool super-bulky weight yarn (60 yds/100g per skein): 18 skeins purple/lavender/blue mix #150
- Size 13 (9mm) 29-inch circular needle
- Size 15 (10mm) 29-inch circular needle or size needed to obtain gauge
- Tapestry needle

6 SUPER BULKY

Gauges
9 sts and 13 rows = 4 inches/10cm in rev St st with larger needle
14-st Leaf Panel = 5¼ inches/ 13.3cm with larger needle
To save time, take time to check gauges.

Pattern Stitch
Leaf Panel (14-st panel)
See Chart.
Row 1 (RS): K3, k2tog, k1, yo, p2, yo, k1, ssk, k3.
Row 2 and all WS rows: P6, k2, p6.
Row 3: K2, k2tog, k1, yo, k1, p2, k1, yo, k1, ssk, k2.
Row 5: K1, k2tog, k1, yo, k2, p2, k2, yo, k1, ssk, k1.
Row 7: K2tog, k1, yo, k3, p2, k3, yo, k1, ssk.
Row 8: Rep Row 2.
Rep Rows 1–8 for Leaf Panel.

Pattern Notes
A circular needle is used to accommodate the large number of stitches. Do not join; turn at the end of each row.

Work first and last st of every row in St st.

Afghan
With smaller needle, cast on 110 sts.
Row 1 (RS): Purl.
Row 2: Knit, and inc one st each end of row. (112 sts)
Next row (RS): With larger needle, k1, work Row 1 of Leaf panel, *p10, work Row 1 of Leaf panel; rep from * 3 times more, end k1.
Next row: P1, work Row 2 of Leaf panel, *k10, work Row 2 of Leaf panel; rep from * 3 times more, end p1.

Work even in pats as established until 21 pat reps are complete.
Next row: With smaller needle, purl across, dec 1 st each end of row. (110 sts)
Next row: Knit.
Bind off all sts loosely.

Upper Border
With RS facing, using smaller needle and beg at upper right corner of afghan, pick up and knit 110 sts across top of afghan.
Knit 3 rows.
Bind off loosely purlwise on RS.

Lower Border
With RS facing, using smaller needle and beg at lower left corner of afghan, pick up and knit 110 sts across bottom of afghan.
Knit 3 rows.
Bind off loosely purlwise on RS.

Side Borders
With RS facing and using smaller needle, pick up and knit 122 sts evenly spaced along side edge of afghan, including upper and lower borders.
Knit 5 rows.
Bind off loosely purlwise on RS. ✥

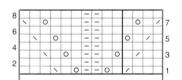

14-st Repeat
LEAF PANEL

STITCH KEY
- ☐ K on RS, p on WS
- ⊟ P on RS, k on WS
- ╱ K2tog
- ╲ Ssk
- ○ Yo

Hand-painted yarn evokes a beautiful summer evening at the seashore.

DESIGN BY LOIS S. YOUNG

Blue Bands Rug

Finished Size

Approx 31 x 49 inches (excluding fringe)

Materials

- Plymouth Encore Chunky 75 percent acrylic/25 percent wool chunky weight yarn (143 yds/100g per ball): 4 balls blue #598 (A)
- Plymouth Encore Colorspun Chunky: 4 balls blue and peach variegated #7123 (B)
- Size 10 (6mm) 29-inch circular needle or size needed to obtain gauge
- Size F/5 (3.75mm) crochet hook

Gauge
14 sts and 26 rows = 4 inches/10 cm in pat
To save time, take time to check gauge.

Pattern Stitch
Row 1 (RS): With B, sl 1, purl to end of row.
Row 2: Sl 1, purl to end of row.
Row 3: Sl 1, knit to end of row. Do not turn, slide sts to other end.
Row 4 (RS): With A, sl 1, purl to end of row.
Row 5: Sl 1, *yo, k2tog; rep from * across. Do not turn, slide sts to other end.
Row 6 (WS): With B, sl 1, knit to end of row.
Row 7: Sl 1, knit to end of row.
Row 8: Sl 1, purl to end of row.
Rows 9–16: Work as for Rows 1–8, exchanging A for B and B for A.
Rep Rows 1–16 for pat.

Pattern Notes
The pattern is made up of 2 eight-row sequences with colors reversed.

Each eight-row sequence is worked with 3 rows of one color, 2 rows of the 2nd color, then 3 rows of the first color. This means that at the end of designated rows, you will not turn the work in the normal fashion; rather, you will slide the stitches back to the other end of the needle and begin the next row with the other color.

Carry yarn not in use up the side.

Rug
With A, cast on 111 sts.

Rows 1 and 2: Sl 1, knit to end of row.
Begin pat st, and work [Rows 1–16] 21 times.
Work Rows 1–8.
Last 2 rows: With A, sl 1, purl to end of row.
Bind off purlwise on RS.

Fringe
Following instructions on page 161, attach fringe as follows: Cut 222 9-inch strands of A. Using crochet hook, attach 2-strands-per-fringe in every other st across end of rug. Trim fringe evenly.

This reversible rug and pillow set is just the thing for leisure-time comfort.

DESIGN BY LOIS S. YOUNG

Blue Bands Floor Pillow

Finished Size

 EASY

Approx 24 x 24 inches

Materials

5 BULKY

- Plymouth Encore Chunky 75 percent acrylic/25 percent wool bulky weight yarn (143 yds/100g per ball): 4 balls blue #598 (A)
- Plymouth EncoreColorspun Chunky: 4 balls blue and peach variegated #7123 (B)
- Size 10 (6mm) 29-inch circular needle or size needed to obtain gauge
- 24-inch square pillow form

Gauge

14 sts and 26 rows = 4 inches/10 cm in pat
To save time, take time to check gauge.

Pattern Stitch

Row 1 (RS): With B, sl 1, purl to end of row.
Row 2: Sl 1, purl to end of row.
Row 3: Sl 1, knit to end of row. Do not turn, slide sts to other end.

Row 4 (RS): With A, sl 1, purl to end of row.
Row 5: Sl 1, *yo, k2tog; rep from * across. Do not turn, slide sts to other end.
Row 6 (WS): With B, sl 1, knit to end of row.
Row 7: Sl 1, knit to end of row.
Row 8: Sl 1, purl to end of row.
Rows 9–16: Work as for Rows 1–8, exchanging A for B and B for A.
Rep Rows 1–16 for pat.

Pattern Notes

The pattern is made up of 2 eight-row sequences with colors reversed.

Each eight-row sequence is worked with 3 rows of one color, 2 rows of the 2nd color, then 3 rows of the first color. This means that at the end of designated rows, you will not turn the work in the normal fashion; rather, you will slide the stitches back to the other end of the needle and begin the next row with the other color.

Carry yarn not in use up the side.

Pillow

Make 2
With B, cast on 87 sts.
Rows 1 and 2: Sl 1, purl to end of row.
Begin Pattern and work [Rows 1–16] 10 times.
Work Rows 1–8.
Last 2 rows: With B, sl 1, purl to end of row.
Bind off purlwise on RS.

Side Borders

With RS facing and B, pick up and knit 4 sts for each 8-row sequence.
Rows 1 (WS) and 2: Sl 1, knit to end of row.
Bind off knitwise on WS.

Assembly

With RS tog, sew pillow pieces together on 3 sides by overcasting through edge sts.

Turn inside out (if desired) and insert pillow form.

Sew rem side. ❧

This fabric looks great on both sides—choose whichever one you want to be on the outside.

DESIGN BY DIANE ZANGL

Wedded Hearts Throw

Finished Size

EASY

Approx 40 x 47 inches

Materials

4 MEDIUM

- Plymouth Encore 75 percent acrylic/25 percent wool medium weight yarn (200 yds/100g per ball): 10 balls natural #146
- Size 7 (4.5mm) 29-inch circular needle or size needed to obtain gauge
- Stitch markers
- Cable needle

Gauge

23 sts and 26 rows = 4 inches/10cm in pat

To save time, take time to check gauge.

Pattern Stitches

Seed St (multiple of 2 sts)
Row 1 (RS): Sl 1, k1, *p1, k1; rep from * across.
Row 2: Sl 1, p1, *k1, p1; rep from * across.
Rep Rows 1 and 2 for pat.
Wedded Hearts and Cables
(multiple of 38 sts + 16 sts)
See Chart on page 106.

Pattern Note

A circular needle is used to accommodate the large number of sts. Do not join; work in rows.

Throw

Cast on 220 sts.

Beg with Row 2, work even in Seed St pat for 7 rows.
Set up row (RS): Work Seed St over 7 sts, pm; work Wedded Hearts and Cables (see Chart) as follows: [work from A to B] 5 times, [B to C] once, pm; work Seed St as established over last 7 sts.

Maintaining 7-st Seed St borders, work 8 complete reps of chart, then work Rows 1–31 once more.
Next row: Work Row 32 of chart, dec 2 sts in each 8-st cable section.

Removing markers, work in Seed St for 6 rows.

Bind off in pat. ✃

Entwined hearts alternate with columns of large and small cables in a romantic wedding gift throw.

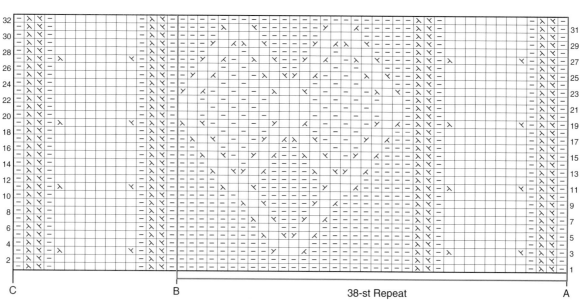

WEDDED HEARTS AND CABLES CHART

STITCH KEY

☐ K on RS, p on WS

– P on RS, k on WS

K 2nd st tbl, k first
st, sl both sts off ndl

Sl 1 to cn and hold in
back, k2, p1 from cn

Sl 2 to cn and hold in
front, p1, k2 from cn

Sl 2 to cn and hold in
back, k2, k2 from cn

Sl 2 cn and hold in
front, k2, k2 from cn

Sl 4 to cn and hold in
back, k4, k4 from cn

High Times Tea Set

DESIGNS BY CHRISTINE L. WALTER

Tea Cozy
Size
Fits a large (8-cups) teapot

Finished Measurement
8 inches tall x 10 inches wide

Materials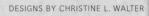
- Plymouth Fantasy Naturale 100 percent mercerized cotton medium weight yarn (140 yds/100g per skein): 1 skein each turquoise #8017 (A) , bright variegated #9951 (B), lavender #6399 (C), and tea green #8011 (D)
- Size 8 (5mm) needles or size needed to obtain gauge
- Stitch holders
- Tapestry needle

Gauge
18 sts and 24 rows = 4 inches/10 cm in Purl-Twist pat
To save time, take time to check gauge.

Special Abbreviation
MB (Make Bobble): Knit into front and back of stitch twice, then knit into front one more time (5 stitches), turn; k5, turn; p5, turn; k5, turn; slip 2nd, 3rd, 4th, and 5th sts over the first st, k1.

Pattern Stitches
A. Bobble Edging (multiple of 6 sts + 5 sts)
Row 1 (RS): K2, * MB, k5, rep from *, end MB, k2.
Rows 2–4: Knit.

B. Purl-Twist Pattern (multiple of 2 sts)
Rows 1 and 3 (RS): Knit.
Row 2: *P2tog, but do not slip from needle; purl first st again, then slip both sts from needle tog; rep from * across.
Row 4: P1, rep from * on Row 2 across to last st, end p1.
Rep Rows 1–4 for pat.

Side
Make 2
With A, cast on 47 sts.
   Work 4 rows of Bobble Edging, dec 1 st on last row. Cut A. (46 sts)
   With B, work Purl-Twist pat, working [4 row rep] 7 times, then work first 2 rows once more. Cut B.

This cheerful tea cozy will add a touch of whimsy to your table while keeping your tea hot longer.

Shape Top
Row 1 (RS): With A, knit.
Row 2: Knit.
Row 3: K2, *k2tog, k2; rep from * across. (35 sts)
Rows 4–8: Knit.
Row 9: K1, *K2tog, k1; rep from * to last st, end k1. (24 sts)
Rows 10–14: Knit.
Row 15: K2tog across. (12 sts)
Rows 16–18: Knit.
Row 19: K2tog across. (6 sts)
Cut A, leaving a long tail. Put sts on holder.

Large Rose
With C and leaving a long tail, cast on 80 sts.
Beg with a RS row, work in St st for 1 inch.
Dec over next three rows as follows:
Row 1: K2tog across. (40 sts)
Row 2: P2tog across. (20 sts)
Row 3: K2tog across. (10 sts)
Cut yarn, leaving a long tail. Using a tapestry needle, thread tail through rem sts, and pull up into gathers. Form rose by twisting the piece round and round from the center, with RS facing out. Pull the rose into shape as you go, letting the fabric roll over. Sew layers together by working a few stitches through all the layers at the bottom to hold them in place.

Small Rose
With C and leaving a long tail, cast on 60 sts.
Beg with a RS row, work in St st for 1 inch.
Dec over next three rows as follows:

Row 1: K2tog across. (30 sts)
Row 2: P2tog across. (15 sts)
Row 3: K2tog across to last st, end k1. (8 sts)
Cut yarn, leaving a long tail. Continue as for large rose.

Leaves
Make 3
With D and leaving long tails, cast on 3 sts.
Row 1 (WS): Purl.
Row 2 (RS): K1, yo, k1, yo, k1. (5 sts)
Row 3 and all WS rows: Purl.
Row 4: K2, yo, k1, yo, k2. (7 sts)
Row 6: K3, yo, k1, yo, k3. (9 sts)
Row 8: K4, yo, k1, yo, k4. (11 sts)
Row 10: Ssk, k7, k2tog. (9 sts)
Row 12: Ssk, k5, k2tog. (7 sts)
Row 14: Ssk, k3, k2tog. (5 sts)
Row 16: Ssk, k1, k2tog. (3 sts)
Row 18: Sk2p.
Cut yarn, and pull through the last st.
Weave in tail at top of leaf, reserving yarn tail at stem end for sewing leaf to cozy.

Assembly
Using a tapestry needle, weave tail at top of the first piece through the live stitches of the 2nd piece and vice versa. Pull tight to close top.
Sew garter portion of cozy at each side of center top.
Place cozy on teapot and mark openings for spout and handle before sewing up sides. Using mattress st, sew sides, leaving sections between markers open.
Sew roses and leaves to center top of tea cozy.

Hot Pads
Finished Measurement
7½ inches square
Materials
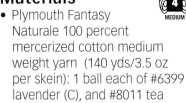
- Plymouth Fantasy Naturale 100 percent mercerized cotton medium weight yarn (140 yds/3.5 oz per skein): 1 ball each of #6399 lavender (C), and #8011 tea green (D)
- Size 8 (5mm) needles or size needed to obtain gauge
- Size H/8 (5mm) crochet hook
- Tapestry needle

Side One
Make 2
With C, cast on 34 sts.
Knit 4 rows.
Change to Purl-Twist pat, and work [4 row rep] 10 times.
Knit 3 rows.
Bind off knitwise on WS.

Side Two
Make 2
Work as for Side One, but bind off until 1 st rem.

Loop
Using crochet hook, chain-10 in last st. Work slip st into first st, then fasten off.

Assembly
With RS facing out, sew the two sides tog.

DESIGNS BY KENNITA TULLY

Little Fringes

Finished Sizes
EASY

Placemat: approx 16½ by 12 inches (excluding fringe)
Glass Cozy: approx 4 inches high and 6¾ inches around (excluding fringe)

Materials
4 MEDIUM

- Plymouth Bella Colour 55 percent cotton/45 percent acrylic medium weight yarn (104 yds/50g per ball): 2 balls blue #17 per set (placemat and glass cozy)
- Size 10 (6mm) needles or size needed to obtain gauge
- Tapestry needle

Gauge
16 sts and 28 rows = 4 inches/ 10cm in St st
To save time, take time to check gauge.

Pattern Notes
Long tail and cable cast-on are used in this pattern (see pages 168 and 171).

The fringes are created by casting on, then immediately binding off 8 sts at each end as indicated.

Placemat
Using long tail method, cast on 84 sts.
Row 1 (WS): Bind off 8 sts, knit across row. (76 sts)
Row 2: Bind off 8 sts, knit across row. (68 sts)
Rows 3 and 5: Purl.
Row 4: Knit.
Row 6: Knit across row; turn and cable cast on 8 sts. (76 sts)
Row 7: Bind off 8 sts, knit across row; turn and cable cast on 8 sts. (76 sts)
Row 8: Bind off 8 sts, knit across row. (68 sts)

Rows 9 and 11: Purl.
Row 10: Knit.
Rep [Rows 6–11] 10 more times.
Work Rows 6 and 7.
Bind off.

Glass Cozy
Using long tail method, cast on 24 sts.
Row 1: Bind off 8 sts, knit across row. (16 sts)
Rows 2 and 4: Knit.
Rows 3 and 5: Purl.
Row 6: Knit across row, turn and cable cast on 8 sts. (24 sts)
Row 7: Bind off 8 sts, knit across row. (16 sts)
Rep [Rows 2–7] 5 more times.
Work Rows 2–5.
Bind off.
Sew cast-on and bind-off edges together.

Nifty fringes are
created as-you-go.
When you're done,
you're DONE!

PAMPERED PETS

Dogs and cats are beloved
members of our families, so
of course we enjoy making
them feel important with
their own beds, wearables
and comfort toys.

DESIGN BY CAROL MAY

Nap Time Cozy

Sizes

BEGINNER

Small (medium, large, extra-large) Instructions are given for smallest size, with larger sizes in parentheses. When only 1 number is given, it applies to all sizes.

Finished Measurements

Width: 12 (16, 20, 24½) inches
Length: 10 (17, 24, 30) inches

Materials

- Plymouth Rimini Rainbow 60 percent acrylic/40 percent wool super bulky weight yarn (38 yds/50 g per ball): 1 (3, 4, 7) balls #31 (A); 1 (2, 3, 5) balls #27 (B)
- Size 15 (10mm) 24-inch circular needle or size needed to obtain gauge
- Additional size 15 (10mm) needle for 3-needle bind off (optional)
- Stitch marker
- Tapestry needle

SUPER BULKY

Gauge

8 sts and 12 rnds = 4 inches/10cm in St st
To save time, take time to check gauge.

Stripe Pattern

Rnd 1: With B, knit.
Rnd 2: With A, knit.
Rep Rnds 1 and 2 for pat.

Blanket

With A, loosely cast on 48 (64, 80, 98) sts.

Join, being careful not to twist stitches, and pm to indicate beg of rnd.

With A, knit 2 rnds.

Work in Stripe pat until piece measures 7 (12, 18, 24) inches from beg. Cut B.

Continue working with A *only* until piece measures 10 (17, 24, 30) inches, or desired length, from beg.

Bind off using method 1 or 2:

1. Loosely bind off all sts, then turn the tube inside out (purl side will be outside) and sew bottom seam.

2. Work 3-needle bind off as follows: holding the circular needle so that both ends are parallel and pointing to the right, use a spare needle to knit 1 st from each point together; *knit the next 2 sts tog (one from each needle), then pull the first st over the 2nd (1 st bound off); rep from * until all sts are bound off.

Turn the bag inside out so that the purl side is on the outside. ❧

Here's an easy-to-knit snuggly blanket created just for your favorite pet!

Home For The Family Dog (Or Feline)

DESIGN BY LOIS S. YOUNG

Finished Sizes

Dog version: Approx 30 x 31 inches

Cat version: Approx 25 x 25 inches

Instructions are given for dog version, with the cat version in parentheses. When only 1 number is given, it applies to both versions.

Materials

- Plymouth Encore 75 percent acrylic/25 percent wool medium weight yarn (200 yds/100g per ball): [Dog version] 3 balls beige #240 (A), 8 balls grey #389 (B); [Cat version] 3 balls pink #241 (A), 6 balls brown #1444 (B)
- Size 7 (4.5 mm) needles or size needed to obtain gauge
- Sharp and blunt point tapestry needles
- Double-bed size extra-loft quilt batting (¾ inch thick)

Gauge

18 sts and 22 rows = 4 inches/ 10cm in St st

To save time, take time to check gauge.

Pattern Notes

Slip the first stitch of each row purlwise; this gives a chain selvage.

Sew all seams by holding WS to WS and overcasting through the chain selvage.

Cushion

Patches

With MC, cast on 27 sts.

Work Dog Chart or Cat Chart.

Dog version: Make 25 squares, 12 with A as MC and B as CC, 13 with B as MC and A as CC.

Cat version: Make 16 squares, 8 with A as MC and B as CC, 8 with B as MC and A as CC.

Sew squares together in checkerboard pattern.

Bottom and sides

With B, cast on 135 (96) sts.

Work 16 rows garter st for one side.

Turning row (RS): Purl.

Continue in garter st until piece measures 31 (25) inches, ending on a WS row. **Note:** *Rows between turning rows form bottom.*

Turning row: Purl.

Work 16 rows of garter st for second side.

Bind off knitwise on WS.

Next Side: *With RS facing, pick up and knit 3 sts for every 4 rows along side of bottom.

Work 16 rows Garter St.

Bind off knitwise on WS.

Rep from * along 4th side of bottom.

Assembly

Sew tog edges of sides to make an "open box" shape.

Cut 4 layers of quilt batting to fit square.

With sharp needle, loosely tack top to batting at each spot where squares intersect.

Place top on top of bottom and sew together.

Run in dryer on air fluff setting for 5 minutes to fluff up batting.

When Fido is tired, he'll be happy to lie down on this cushy quilt. Don't worry— Fluffy has her very own cushion too!

DOG CHART

STITCH & COLOR KEY
☐ With MC, K on RS, p on WS
▨ With CC, P on RS, k on WS
⌒ With MC, sl 1 purlwise
– With MC, K on WS

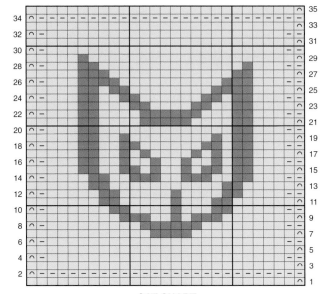

CAT CHART

STITCH & COLOR KEY
☐ With MC, K on RS, p on WS
▨ With CC, P on RS, k on WS
⌒ With MC, sl 1 purlwise
– With MC, K on WS

DESIGN BY BONNIE FRANZ

Strut Your Stuff

Sizes

EASY

Dog's small (medium, large) Instructions are given for smallest size, with larger sizes in parentheses. When only 1 number is given, it applies to all sizes.

Finished Measurements

Back width: 13 (16, 19) inches
Length: 13 (17½, 22) inches

Materials

3 LIGHT

- Plymouth Encore D.K. 75 percent acrylic/25 percent wool light weight yarn (150 yds/50g per ball): 2 (2, 3) balls orange #1383
- Size 5 (3.75mm) needles or size needed to obtain gauge
- Tapestry needle
- 3 (⅞-inch) buttons

Gauge

17 sts and 12 rows (1 full repeat of pat) = 3 x 1½ inches
To save time, take time to check gauge.

Pattern Stitch

Ridged Old Shale (multiple of 17 sts)
Rows 1-3: Knit.
Row 4 (WS): Purl.
Row 5: *[K2tog] 3 times, [yo, k1] 5 times, yo, [ssk] 3 times; rep from * across.
Row 6: Purl.
Row 7: Knit.
Row 8: Purl.
Row 9: Rep Row 5.
Row 10: Purl.
Rows 11 and 12: Knit.
Rep Rows 1-12 for pat.

Dog Sweater

Back

Cast on 68 (85, 102) sts.
Work in Ridged Old Shale until piece measures 12 (16½, 21) inches from beg.
Bind off 62 (75, 87) sts, knit to end. (6, 10, 15 sts)

Chest band

Work in garter st on rem sts until band measures 6 (8, 10) inches or length needed to reach around upper chest comfortably.
Bind off.

Side edges

Right edge: Pick up and knit 68 (92, 116) sts. Knit 4 rows. Bind off.
Left edge: Pick up and knit 68 (92, 116) sts. Knit 4 rows.
Bind off 24 (33, 40) sts at beg of next 2 rows. (20, 26, 36 sts)

Belly band

Work even in garter st until band measures 3½ (5, 6) inches or length needed to reach around belly of dog.
Bind off all sts.

Finishing

Sew 2 buttons on Belly band and 1 button on Chest band.
Use openings in lace pattern as buttonholes.

Lady will be sitting pretty in her easy lace-knit sweater.

DESIGN BY BONNIE FRANZ

Cruising The Neighborhood

Sizes

EASY

Dog's small (medium, large) Instructions are given for smallest size, with larger sizes in parentheses. When only 1 number is given, it applies to all sizes.

Finished Measurements

Back width: 14 (17, 20) inches
Length: 15 (19¾, 24¾) inches

Materials

5 BULKY

- Plymouth Encore Chunky 75 percent acrylic/25 percent wool bulky weight yarn (143 yds/100g per skein): 1 (2, 2) skein navy #658 (MC), 1 skein (5mm) grey #678 (CC)
- Size 8 (5mm) circular needles at least 24 inches long
- Size 10 (6mm) circular needle at least 24 inches long, or size needed to obtain gauge
- Tapestry needle
- 3 (⅞-inch) buttons

Gauge

13 sts and 18 rows = 4 inches/10cm in St st with larger needles
To save time, take time to check gauge.

Stripe Pattern

Work following sequence in St st:
5 rows MC, 1 row CC
Rep these 6 rows for pat.

Pattern Notes

This sweater is worked from side to side.

The circular needle allows you to work the Stripe Pattern from either side of fabric depending on where the necessary yarn is.

Dog Sweater

Back

Using smaller needles and MC, cast on 42 (58, 74) sts.
Knit 3 rows.

Buttonhole row: K16 (20, 26), k2tog, yo, knit to last 18 (22, 28) sts, yo, k2tog, knit to end of row.
Knit 3 rows.

Change to larger needles, and work even in St st and Stripe pat until piece measures 11 (14, 17) inches from beg.

Change to smaller needles and MC, and knit 6 rows.

Belly band

Bind off 14 (18, 24) sts, k14 (18, 22), bind off rem 14 (18, 24) sts.

Work rem 14 (18, 22) sts in garter st until band measures approx 3½ (5, 6) inches or length needed to reach around belly of dog.
Bind off all sts.

Back and front edges

*With smaller needles and MC, pick up and knit 44 (58, 71) sts across back edge of sweater.
Knit 6 rows.*
Bind off all sts.
Rep from * to * across front edge of sweater.

Chest strap

Next row: Bind off 38 (48, 56) sts, knit to end of row.

Continue in garter st until strap measures 6 (8, 10) inches, or length needed to reach around upper chest comfortably.

Buttonhole row: K2 (3, 4), yo, k2tog, knit to end of row.
Knit 4 rows.
Bind off all sts.

Finishing

Sew 2 buttons on Belly band and 1 button on Chest strap opposite buttonholes.

Spot will step out in style in his business-like sweater. Going to the park? It's also perfect for a doggie play-date.

DESIGNS BY BONNIE FRANZ

Felted Pet Toys

Balls

Finished Size
Circumference:
Approx 7½ inches

INTERMEDIATE

Materials
- Plymouth Galway Worsted 100 percent wool medium weight yarn (210 yds/100g per ball): 1 ball each in green #127 (A) and pink #135 (B) **Note:** *One skein of each color will be plenty to make several balls.*

4 MEDIUM

5 BULKY

- Size 10½ (7mm) double-pointed needles or size needed to obtain gauge
- Tapestry needle
- Non-felting stuffing material (pantyhose work well)

Gauge
16 sts and 20 rnds = 4 inches/ 10cm in St st (pre-felting)
To save time, take time to check gauge.

Special Abbreviation
Inc 1 (Increase 1): Knit into the stitch in the row below the stitch on the LH needle.

Solid Colored Ball
With A or B, cast on 5 sts and distribute among 3 needles.
  Join, being careful not to twist sts, and pm to indicate beg of rnd.
Rnd 1: *Inc 1, k1; rep from * around. (10 sts)
Rnd 2 and all even rounds: Knit.
Rnd 3: *Inc 1, k2; rep from * around. (15 sts)

Rnd 5: *Inc 1, k3; rep from * around. (20 sts)
Rnd 7: *Inc 1, k4; rep from * around. (25 sts)
Rnd 9: *Inc 1, k5; rep from * around. (30 sts)
Rnd 11: *Inc 1, k6; rep from * around. (35 sts)
Rnd 13: Knit.
Rnd 15: *K2tog, k5; rep from * around. (30 sts)
Rnd 17: *K2tog, k4; rep from * around. (25 sts)
Rnd 19: *K2tog, k3; rep from * around. (20 sts)
Rnd 21: *K2tog, k2; rep from * around. (15 sts)

Rnd 23: *K2tog, k1; rep from * around. (10 sts)
Rnd 25: *K2tog; rep from * around. (5 sts)
  Cut yarn leaving a 6-inch tail.

Finishing
Using a tapestry needle, draw tail loosely through rem sts. Do not tighten.
  Stuff ball.
  Run tail through sts once more, pull tight, and fasten securely.
  Work in ends.

Felting Instructions
  Place finished balls in pillowcase and put in washing machine with a small amount of soap and a pair of jeans (important for agitation).

The bone is just for Doggie, but the balls would be fun for kids and babies too!

Run the machine, set for the smallest load, and hot wash/cold rinse. Remove the balls and check size. Reset wash/rinse cycle, if necessary, for additional felting.

When desired size has been reached, remove the balls. Dry in dryer.

Variations:

Two-tone: Work to Rnd 13 with A, then change to B for remainder of ball.

Center stripe: Work to Rnd 11 with A, work 3 rnds with B, work remainder of ball with A.

Stripes: Alternate 2 rnds A with 2 rnds B throughout piece.

Felted Bone
Finished Size
Approx 8 x 4 inches at widest points

Materials
- Plymouth Galway Chunky 100% wool bulky weight yarn (123 yds/100g per ball): 1 ball white #01
- Small amount of contrast yarn for sewing
- Size 13 (9mm) needles or size needed to obtain gauge
- Sharp-pointed tapestry needle
- Non-felting stuffing material (pantyhose work well)
- "Squeaker" available at some pet or notions stores (optional)

Gauge
10 sts and 28 rows = 4 inches/10 cm in St st (pre-felting)
To save time, take time to check gauge.

Bone
Cast on 50 sts.
Work 30 rows in St st.
Bind off loosely.
Work in ends.

Finishing
Felt as for balls above.

When piece is completely dry, cut 2 bone shapes from felt using pattern given.

Using buttonhole stitch (page 163) and contrast yarn, sew pieces around outside leaving one end open.

Stuff piece and insert squeaker (if desired); complete working the buttonhole stitch around end. Bury thread ends inside bone. ✍

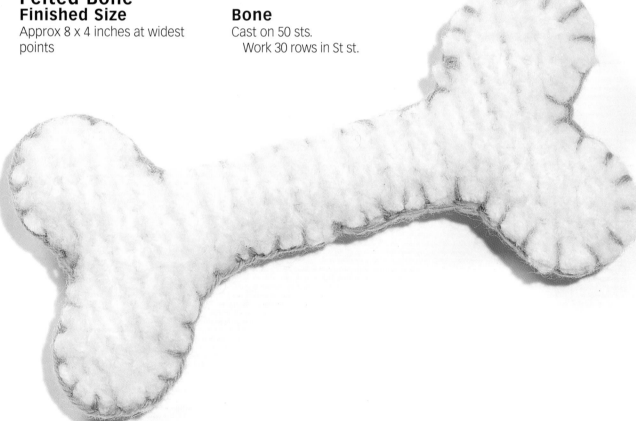

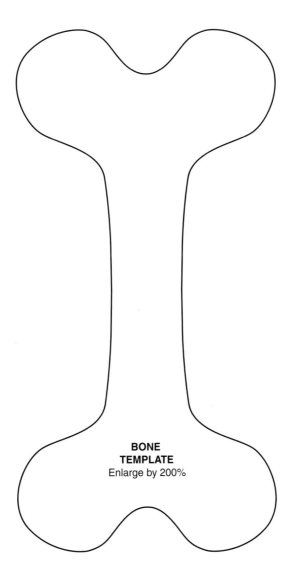

**BONE
TEMPLATE**
Enlarge by 200%

CHRISTMAS TIME

This most wonderful and busiest season of the year is time to celebrate family style. We've included festive decorations and quick gift ideas to please all.

Perfect Gift Purse

DESIGN BY DIANE ELLIOTT

Finished Size

INTERMEDIATE

Approx 10 x 11 inches, after felting

Materials

- Plymouth Galway Worsted 100 percent wool medium weight yarn (218 yds/100g per ball): 1 ball pink #114 (A)
- Plymouth Outback Mohair 70 percent mohair/26 percent wool/4 percent nylon bulky weight yarn (220 yds/100g per skein): 1 skein pink-orange-turquoise variegated #895 (B)
- Size 10½ 16-inch circular needle or size needed to obtain gauge
- Stitch markers (2 different colors)
- Sharp-pointed tapestry needle
- Heavy sewing thread to match purse
- Mohair brush (or any stiff bristle brush)

Gauge

17 sts and 22 rnds = 4 inches/10cm in St st with A (pre-felting)
To save time, take time to check gauge.

Pattern Stitch

Garter stitch (in-the-round)
Rnd 1: Knit.
Rnd 2: Purl.
Rep Rnds 1 and 2 for pat.

Special Abbreviations

Inc 1 (Increase 1): On knit rnds, knit in front and back of stitch; on purl rnds, purl in front and back of stitch.

Pattern Notes

Do not cut yarn not in use; carry unused yarn up the piece, wrapping around yarn in use every 2 or 3 rnds.

Base and handles are worked using both yarns held together.

Purse

Base

With A, cast on 60 sts. Join, being careful not to twist sts, and pm to indicate beg of rnd.

Rnd 1: With A and B held tog, k30, place different-colored marker to indicate side edge, k30.

Knit inc rnd: *Sl marker, inc 1, knit to 1 st before marker, inc 1; rep from * once more. (64 sts)

Purl inc rnd: *Sl marker, inc 1, purl to 1 st before marker, inc 1; rep from * once more. (68 sts)

Rep [last 2 rnds] 3 more times. (100 sts)

Sides

Next 10 rnds: With A, knit.
Next 10 rnds: With B, work in garter st.
Dec rnd: With A, slip marker, k2tog, knit to 2 sts before marker, ssk; rep from * once more. (96 sts)
Next 8 rnds: Knit.
Next 10 rnds: With B, work in garter st.
Next 8 rnds: With A, work Dec rnd, then knit 7 rnds. (92 sts)
Next 8 rnds: With B, work 8 rnds in garter st.
Next 7 rnds: With A, work Dec rnd, then knit 6 rnds. (88 sts)
Next 8 rnds: With B, work 8 rnds in garter st.

Next 6 rnds: With A, work Dec rnd, then knit 5 rnds. (84 sts)

Handles

Next 2 rnds: With A and B held tog, work 2 rnds in garter st.
Next rnd: K14, bind off 14 sts, k28, bind off 14 sts, k14.
Next rnd: P14, cast on 14 sts, p28, cast on 14 sts, p14.

With A and B held tog, continue working in garter st for 1¾ inches, ending with knit rnd.

Bind off all sts knitwise.

Assembly

Sew bottom seam. Weave in any ends.

Pocket

With A, cast on 21 sts.
Knit 3 rows.
Next row (WS): K1, p19, k1.
Next row: Knit.

Rep last 2 rows until piece measures 6½ inches, ending with a RS row.

Knit 1 more row. Bind off.

Felting Instructions

Place finished purse and pocket piece in separate pillowcases and place in washing machine with a small amount of soap and a pair of jeans (important for agitation). Run the machine set for the smallest load and hot water wash. Check on the pieces every 5 minutes or so.

Remove the pieces and check the size. Reset wash cycle if necessary, to increase agitation

CONTINUED ON PAGE 148

Garter-stitch bands of variegated mohair provide soft texture and liven up this pretty pink handbag. There's even a key pocket inside.

DESIGN BY CHRISTINE L. WALTER

Socks With a Twinkle

Size

INTERMEDIATE

Woman's small/medium (approx 8-inch circumference foot)

Materials

- Plymouth Sockotta 45 percent cotton/40 percent superwash wool/15 percent nylon fine weight yarn (414 yds/100g per ball): 1 ball #26
- Size 2 (2.75mm) double-pointed needles (set of 5) or size needed to obtain gauge
- Size 6/0 seed beads: 50 each in crystal silver lined (A), fuchsia silver lined (B), crystal yellow lined (C) and crystal hot pink lined (D), or colors of your choice
- Beading needle

1 SUPER FINE

Gauge

32 sts and 42 rnds = 4 inches/10 cm in St st
To save time, take time to check gauge.

Special Abbreviations

BUB (Bring Up Bead): Slide a bead up against the stitch just worked.
N1, N2, N3, N4: Needle 1, needle 2, needle 3, needle 4

Pattern Stitch

Beaded Rib (multiple of 12 sts)
Rnds 1 and 2: *K2, p2; rep from * around.
Rnd 3: *[K2, p2] twice, k2, p1, BUB, p1; rep from * around.
Rnds 4–6: Rep Rnd 1.
Rnd 7: *K2, p1, BUB, p1, [k2, p2] twice; rep from * around.

Rnds 8–10: Rep Rnd 1.
Rnd 11: *K2, p2, k2, p1, BUB, p1, k2, p2; rep from * around.
Rnd 12: Rep Rnd 1.
Rep Rnds 1–12 for pat.

Pattern Note

Slip all slipped sts purlwise.

Socks

Leg

Using beading needle, string 80 beads on yarn in sequence A-B-C-D, or as desired, and push down.

Leaving a tail long enough for casting on, make slip-knot for long-tailed cast-on (page 168) and put on needle. String 20 more beads on tail.

Cast on 1 st, BUB, *cast on 3 sts, BUB; rep from * 18 times more, end BUB, cast on 1 st. (60 sts)

Divide sts evenly on 4 dpns.

Join, being careful not to twist sts.

Mark the first needle: this is N1 and the beg of the rnd.

Work in Beaded Rib until all beads have been used. Work 2 more rnds in k2, p2 rib.

Heel flap

At beg of next rnd, transfer sts from N3 to N4, turn. (30 sts on N4)

Work Heel st as follows:
Row 1 (WS): Sl 1, purl across.
Row 2: *Sl 1, k1; rep from * across.
Rep Rows 1 and 2 for a total of 28 rows, then work Row 1 once more.

Turn square heel

Note: Keep working heel sts as you turn the heel.
Row 1 (RS): *Sl 1, k1; rep from *

9 more times, ssk, turn. (8 sts rem unworked)
Row 2: Sl 1, p8, p2tog, turn. (8 sts rem unworked)
Row 3: *Sl 1, k1; rep from * 3 more times, sl 1, ssk, turn. (7 sts rem unworked)
Row 4: Sl 1, p8, p2tog, turn. (7 sts rem unworked)

Continue working in this manner, repeating Rows 3 and 4 until all sts have been worked. (10 sts rem)

Set up gusset

Next rnd: With RS facing, knit across heel sts using empty dpn as follows: Sl 1, k4; with another needle (N1), k5, pick up and knit 15 sts along left side of flap; with N2, work 15 instep sts in pat as established; with N3, work rem 15 instep sts in pat as established; with N4, pick up and knit 15 sts along right side of flap, k5 sts from first dpn. Beg of rnd is in center of heel flap. (70 sts divided as follows: N1: 20 sts; N2: 15 sts; N3: 15 sts; N4: 20 sts)

Shape Gusset

Rnd 1: N1: Knit to last 3 sts, k2tog, k1; N2 and N3 (instep): work across in pat as established; N4: k1, ssk, knit to end of rnd.
Rnd 2: N1: Knit; N2 and N3: work across in pat as established; N4: knit.
Rep Rnds 1 and 2 until 60 sts rem. (15 sts on each needle)

Foot

Work even until foot measures 2 inches less than desired length.

CONTINUED ON PAGE 148

These lovely lavender and chocolate colored cotton socks are embellished with complementary shades of sparkling beads, adding a little elegance to your feet anytime you get to rest and put them up.

DESIGN BY CHRISTINE L. WALTER

Wintry Wishes

Finished Sizes

INTERMEDIATE

Hat circumference:
Approx 20 inches
Scarf: Approx 63 x 6¾ inches

Materials

- Plymouth Galway Worsted 100 percent wool medium weight yarn (210 yds/100g per ball): 3 balls of cornflower blue #83 for scarf; 1 ball for hat
- **Hat:** Size 7 (4.5mm) 16-inch circular needle and set of double-pointed needles or size to obtain gauge
- **Scarf:** Size 7 (4.5mm) straight needles or size needed to obtain gauge
- Cable needle
- Tapestry needle

Gauge

28 sts and 27 rows = 4 inches/10 cm in pattern stitch
To save time, take time to check gauge.

Special Abbreviations

C2B (Cross 2 Back): Sl 1 to cn and hold in back, k1, k1 from cn.
C2BW (Cross 2 Back on WS): Sl 1 to cn and hold in back, p1, p1 from cn.
C2F (Cross 2 Front): Sl 1 to cn and hold in front, k1, k1 from cn.
C2FW (Cross 2 Front on WS): Sl 1 to cn and hold in front, p1, p1 from cn.
C3F (Cable 3 Front): Sl 1 to cn and hold in front, k2, k1 from cn.
Cl 10 (Cluster 10): [K2, p2] twice, k2, slip these 10 sts to cn; wrap yarn 3 times counter-clockwise around sts on cn; slip sts back to RH needle.
M1 (Make 1): Insert tip of LH needle under horizontal strand between st just worked and next st and knit through back loop.
M1P (Make 1 Purlwise): Insert tip of LH needle under horizontal strand between st just worked and next st and purl through back loop.

Pattern Note

A chart for the pattern stitch is included on page 136 for those preferring to work from a chart.

Scarf

Note: Wheat Sheaves pattern is a multiple of 17 sts (expanding to 25 sts) + 14.
Cast on 48 sts.

Wheat Sheaves

Row 1 (RS): [P2, k2] 3 times, p2; *C3L, [p2, k2] 3 times, p2; rep from * to end. (17 sts in rep)
Row 2: [K2, p2] 3 times, k2; *p3; [k2, p2] 3 times, k2; rep from * to end.
Row 3: [P2, k2] 3 times, p2; *M1P, k1, p1, k1, M1, [p2, k2] 3 times, p2; rep from * to end. (19 sts in rep)
Row 4: [K2, p2] 3 times, k2; *C2FW, k1, C2BW; [k2, p2] 3 times, k2; rep from * to end.
Row 5: [P2, k2] 3 times, p2; *M1P, [k1, p1] twice, k1, M1P, [p2, k2] 3 times, p2; rep from * to end. (21 sts in rep)
Row 6: [K2, p2] 3 times, k2; *C2FW, k1, p1, k1, C2BW, [k2, p2] 3 times, k2; rep from * to end.
Row 7: [P2, k2] 3 times, p2; *M1P, [k1, p1] 3 times, k1, M1P, [p2, k2] 3 times, p2; rep from * to end. (23 sts in rep)
Row 8: [K2, p2] 3 times, k2; *C2FW, [k1, p1] twice, k1, C2BW, [k2, p2] 3 times, k2; rep from * to end.
Row 9: [P2, k2] 3 times, p2; *M1P, [k1, p1] 4 times, k1, M1P, [p2, k2] 3 times, p2; rep from * to end. (25 sts in rep)
Row 10: [K2, p2] 3 times, k2; *C2FW, [k1, p1] 3 times, k1, C2BW, [k2, p2] 3 times, k2; rep from * to end.
Row 11: P2, Cl 10, p2; *[k1, p1] 5 times, k1, p2, Cl 10, p2; rep from * to end.
Row 12: [K2, p2] 3 times, k2; *[p1, k1] 5 times, p1, [k2, p2] 3 times, k2; rep from * to end.
Row 13: [P2, k2] 3 times, p2; *ssk, [p1, k1] 3 times, p1, k2tog, [p2, k2] 3 times, p2; rep from * to end. (23 sts in rep)
Row 14: [K2, p2] 3 times, k2; *[p1, k1] 4 times, p1, [k2, p2] 3 times, k2; rep from * to end.
Row 15: [P2, k2] 3 times, p2; *ssk, [p1, k1] twice, p1, k2tog, [p2, k2] 3 times, p2; rep from * to end. (21 sts in rep)
Row 16: [K2, p2] 3 times, k2; *[p1, k1] 3 times, p1, [k2, p2] 3 times, k2; rep from * to end.
Row 17: [P2, k2] 3 times, p2; *ssk, p1, k1, p1, k2tog, [p2, k2] 3 times, p2; rep from * to end. (19 sts in rep)
Row 18: [K2, p2] 3 times, k2; *[p1, k1] twice, p1, [k2, p2] 3 times, k2; rep from * to end.
Row 19: [P2, k2] 3 times, p2; *ssk, p1, k2tog, [p2, k2)] 3 times, p2; rep from * to end. (17 sts in rep)
Row 20: [K2, p2] 3 times, k2; *p1,

This hat and scarf set is warm, thick, and cozy. The wheat sheaves design gives this set a wonderful texture that appeals to the eye and at the same time creates a fabric that looks great on both sides.

k1, p1, [k2, p2] 3 times, k2; rep from * to end.

Rep Wheat Sheaves pat 20 more times or to desired length, ending on Row 20.

Bind off in pattern by working Row 1.

Hat

Note: *Wheat Sheaves pattern is a multiple of 17 sts (expanding to 25 sts).*
Cast on 136 sts.

Join, being careful not to twist sts, and pm to indicate beg of rnd.

Wheat Sheaves

Rnd 1: *[P2, k2] 3 times, p2, C3L; rep from * around. (17 sts in rep)
Rnd 2: *[P2, k2] 3 times, p2, k3; rep from * around.
Rnd 3: *[P2, k2] 3 times, p2, M1, k1, p1, k1, M1; rep from * around. (19 sts in rep)
Rnd 4: *[P2, k2] 3 times, p2, C2F, p1, C2B; rep from * around.
Rnd 5: *[P2, k2] 3 times, p2, M1, [k1, p1] twice, k1, M1; rep from * around. (21 sts in rep)
Rnd 6: *[P2, k2] 3 times, p2, C2F, p1, k1, p1, C2B; rep from * around.
Rnd 7: *[P2, k2] 3 times, p2, M1, [k1, p1] 3 times, k1, M1; rep from * around. (23 sts in rep)
Rnd 8: *[P2, k2] 3 times, p2, C2F, [p1, k1] twice, p1, C2B; rep from * around.

Rnd 9: *[P2, k2] 3 times, p2, M1, [k1, p1] 4 times, k1, M1; rep from * around. (25 sts in rep)
Rnd 10: *[P2, k2] 3 times, p2, C2F, [p1, k1] 3 times, p1, C2B; rep from * around.
Rnd 11: *P2, Cl 10, p2, [k1, p1] 5 times, k1; rep from * around.
Rnd 12: *[P2, k2] 3 times, p2, [k1, p1] 5 times, k1; rep from * around.
Rnd 13: *[P2, k2] 3 times, p2, ssk, [p1, k1] 3 times, p1, k2tog; rep from * around. (23 sts in rep)
Rnd 14: *[P2, k2] 3 times, p2, [k1, p1] 4 times, k1; rep from * around.
Rnd 15: *[P2, k2] 3 times, p2, ssk, [p1, k1] twice, p1, k2tog; rep from * around. (21 sts in rep)
Rnd 16: *[P2, k2] 3 times, p2, [k1, p1] 3 times, k1; rep from * around.
Rnd 17: *[P2, k2] 3 times, p2, ssk, p1, k1, p1, k2tog; rep from * around. (19 sts in rep)
Rnd 18: *[P2, k2] 3 times, p2, [k1, p1] twice, k1; rep from * around.
Rnd 19: *[P2, k2] 3 times, p2, ssk, p1, k2tog; rep from * around. (17 sts in rep)
Rnd 20: *[P2, k2] 3 times, p2, k1, p1, k1; rep from * around.

Rep Wheat Sheaves pat once more, then work Rnd 1 again.

Shape crown

Rnd 1: *P2, k2, p1, k2tog, ssk, p1, k2, p2, k1, k2tog; rep from * around. (112 sts)

Rnd 2: *P2, k2, p1, k2, p1, k2, p2, k2; rep from * around.
Rnd 3: *P2, k2, k2tog, ssk, k2, p2, k2; rep from * around. (96 sts)
Rnd 4: *P2, k6, p2, k2; rep from * around.
Rnd 5: *P2, k1, k2tog, ssk, k1, p2, k2; rep from * to end of rnd. (80 sts)
Rnd 6: *P2, k4, p2, k2; rep from * around.
Rnd 7: *P2, k2tog, ssk, p2, k2; rep from * around. (64 sts)
Rnd 8: *P2, K2; rep from * around.
Rnd 9: *P1, k2tog, ssk, p1, k2; rep from * around. (48 sts)
Rnd 10: *P1, K2; rep from * around.
Rnd 11: *K2tog, ssk, k2; rep from * around. (32 sts)
Rnd 12: Knit.
Rnd 13: *K2, k2tog; rep from * around. (24 sts)
Rnd 14: Knit.
Rnd 15: *K1, k2tog, rep from * to end of rnd. (16 sts)
Rnd 16: *K2tog, rep from * to end of rnd. (8 sts)

Finishing

Break yarn leaving an 8-inch tail.

Using tapestry needle, pass tail through rem sts twice and pull tight. ✍

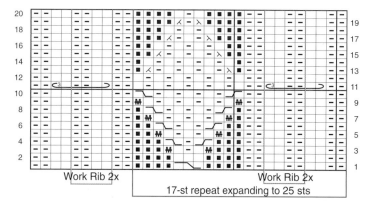

Work Rib 2x   Work Rib 2x
17-st repeat expanding to 25 sts

WHEAT SHEAVES CHART

STITCH KEY

□ K on RS, p on WS
– P on RS, k on WS
■ No stitch
⋋ Ssk
⋌ K2tog
Ⓜ M1P
⌐ C2B or C2BW
⌐ C2F or C2FW
⌐ C3F
⌐⌐ Cl10

Note: For scarf, work chart back and forth. For hat, work chart starting at the right edge on every rnd.

DESIGN BY GAYLE BUNN

Cabled With Love

Finished Measurements

INTERMEDIATE

5 BULKY

Woman's scarf: Approx 7½ x 66 inches (excluding fringe)

Man's scarf: Approx 7½ x 67 inches

Hat circumference: 22 inches

Materials

- Plymouth Baby Alpaca Grande 100 percent superfine baby alpaca bulky weight yarn (110 yds/100g per skein): 4 skeins wheat #401 (man's) *or* slate #202 (woman's) for both hat and scarf
- Size 10½ (6.5mm) needles or size needed to obtain gauge
- Cable needle
- Medium size crochet hook for attaching fringe
- Tapestry needle

Gauge

13 sts and 18 rows = 4 inches/ 10cm in Moss st
To save time, take time to check gauge.

Special Abbreviations

C3F (Cable 3 Front): Sl 2 to cn and hold in front, p1, k2 from cn.

C3B (Cable 3 Back): Sl 1 to cn and hold in back, k2, p1 from cn.

C4F (Cable 4 Front): Sl 2 to cn and hold in front, k2, k2 from cn.

C4B (Cable 4 Back): Sl 2 to cn and hold in back, k2, k2 from cn.

M1 (Make 1): Insert tip of LH needle under horizontal strand between st just worked and next st and k1-tbl.

SK2P (left-leaning double decrease): Sl 1, k2tog, psso.

Pattern Stitches

A. Moss Stitch

(odd number of sts)

Row 1 (WS): *K1, p1; rep from *, ending k1.

Row 2: Rep Row 1.

Row 3: *P1, k1; rep from *, ending p1.

Row 4: Rep Row 3.
Rep Rows 1-4 for pat.

B. Braided Cable

(13 st panel)

Row 1 (WS): K3, p4, k2, p2, k2.

Row 2: P2, C3F, C3B, C3F, p2.

Row 3: K2, p2, k2, p4, k3.

Row 4: P3, C4B, p2, k2, p2.

Row 5: Rep Row 3.

Row 6: P2, C3B, C3F, C3B, p2.

Row 7: Rep Row 1.

Row 8: P2, k2, p2, C4F, p3.
Rep Rows 1–8 for pat.

Pattern Note

A chart for the Braided Cable pattern is included on page 139 for those preferring to work from a chart.

Scarf

Man's Version only

Cast on 24 sts.

Rows 1–3: Knit.

Row 4: K9, M1, *k3, M1; rep from * once more, knit to end. (27 sts)

Woman's Version only

Cast on 27 sts.

Both Versions:

Setup row (WS): Work 7 sts in Moss St, work Row 1 of Braided Cable, work 7 sts in Moss St. Continue in pats as established until piece measures approx 66 inches from beg, or desired length, ending on Row 3 of Braided Cable.

This luxurious baby alpaca cabled set will keep your loved one warm on cold wintry days.

Man's Version only:
Next row (RS): K9, k2tog, *k2, k2tog; rep from * once more, k9. (24 sts)
Next 2 rows: Knit.
Bind off knitwise on WS.
Woman's Version only:
Bind off in pat.

Fringe
Following Fringe instructions on page 161, make Single Knot fringe.
Cut 54 lengths of yarn, each approx 12 inches long. Holding 3 strands per fringe and using a crochet hook, attach 9 evenly spaced fringes to each end of scarf. Trim ends evenly.

Hat
Leaving a 20-inch tail, cast on 74 sts.
Row 1: *K2, p2; rep from * to last 2 sts, k2.
Row 2: *P2, k2; rep from * to last 2 sts, p2.
Continue in rib as established until work measures 4½ inches, ending with Row 2.
Next row (RS): Rib across 34 sts, [M1, rib 2] 3 times, rib to end. (77 sts)

Set up Moss Stitch and Braided Cable
Rows 1 and 2: Work 31 sts in Moss st, p1, work Braided Cable, p1, work 31 sts in Moss st.
Rows 3 and 4: Work 31 sts in Moss st, k1, work Braided Cable, k1, work 31 sts in Moss st.
Continue in pats as established until work measures approx 8 (8¾ for man's) inches from beg, ending with Row 1 of Moss st.

Shape crown
Next row (RS): [K1, p3tog] 8 times, work in pat as established to last 32 sts, [p3tog, k1] 8 times. (45 sts)
Next 5 rows: Work even in pat as established.
Next row (RS): [P1, SK2P] 4 times, work in pat as established to last 16 sts, [SK2P, p1] 4 times. (29 sts)
Next row: Work even in pat as established.
Next row: [K2tog] 14 times, k1. (15 sts)
Cut yarn, leaving an 8-inch tail.
Using a tapestry needle, draw tail through rem sts, pull tight, and fasten securely.
Using a tapestry needle and cast on tail, and with WS facing, sew half of rib seam (turn-back cuff).
Turn work RS out. With RS facing, complete seam.

Woman's Version only:
Pompom
Wind yarn around 4 fingers approx 50 times. Remove from fingers and tie tightly around center of loops. Cut through each end. Trim evenly. Sew to top of Hat.

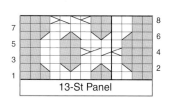
BRAIDED CABLE CHART
13-St Panel

STITCH KEY
K on RS, p on WS
P on RS, K on WS
C3F
C3B
C4B
C4F

Candy Canes & Holly

DESIGN BY CHRISTINE L. WALTER

Finished Size

Approx 37½ x 20 inches

INTERMEDIATE

Materials

- Plymouth Galway Worsted 100 percent wool medium weight yarn (210 yds/100g per ball): 3 balls of Christmas red #16 (A), 1 ball cream #01 (B), 1 ball green #17 (C)
- Size 8 (5mm) 24-inch circular and double-pointed needles or size needed to obtain gauge
- Spare circular needles or waste yarn for stitch holders
- Stitch markers
- Tapestry needle

Gauge

19 sts and 25 rows = 4 inches/10 cm in St st
To save time, take time to check gauge.

Special Abbreviation

Inc 1 (Increase 1): Knit in front and back of st.

Pattern Stitches

A. Zig Zag Lace (multiple of 11 sts + 1)
Row 1 (WS) and every WS row: Purl.
Row 2: *K3, p3, k2tog, yo, k3; rep from *, end last rep k4.
Row 4: *K2, p3, k2tog, yo, k4; rep from *, end last rep k5.
Row 6: *K1, p3, k2tog, yo, k5; rep from *, end last rep k6.
Row 8: *K4, yo, ssk, p3, k2; rep from *, end last rep k3.
Row 10: *K5, yo, ssk, p3, k1; rep from *, end last rep k2.

Row 12: *K6, yo, ssk, p3; rep from *, end last rep k1.
Rep Rows 1-12 for pat.

B. Candy Cane Lace (multiple of 8 sts + 3)
Row 1 (WS) and every WS row: Purl.
Row 2: K3, *ssk, yo, k1, yo, k2tog, k3; rep from *.
Row 4: K2, *ssk, yo, k3, yo, k2tog, k1; rep from *, end last rep k2.
Row 6: K5, *ssk, yo, k6; rep from *, end last rep k4.
Row 8: K4, *ssk, yo, k6; rep from *, end last rep k5.
Row 10: K3, *ssk, yo, k6; rep from * across.
Row 12: K2, *ssk, yo, k6; rep from *, end last rep k7.

C. Lace Diamond Border (multiple of 8 sts + 2)
Row 1 (RS): K1, *k1, yo, k3, pass 3rd st on RH needle over first 2 sts; rep from *, ending k1.
Row 2 and every WS row: Purl.
Row 3: Knit.
Row 5: *K4, yo, ssk, k2; rep from * to last 2 sts, k2.
Row 7: *K3, [yo, ssk] twice, k1; rep from * to last 2 sts, k2.
Row 9: *K2, [yo, ssk] 3 times; rep from * to last 2 sts, k2.
Row 11: Rep Row 7.
Row 13: Rep Row 5.
Row 15: Knit.
Row 17: Rep Row 1.
Row 18: Purl.

D. Slanted Eyelet Edging (8 sts expanding to 12 sts)
Row 1: Sl 1, k1, [yo, k2tog] twice, yo, k2. (9 sts)
Rows 2, 4, 6, and 8 (RS): Sl 1, knit to last st, p2tog (last st with 1

st from runner).
Row 3: Sl 1, k2, [yo, k2tog] twice, yo, k2. (10 sts)
Row 5: Sl 1, k3, [yo, k2tog] twice, yo, k2. (11 sts)
Row 7: Sl 1, k4, [yo, k2tog] twice, yo, k2. (12 sts)
Row 9: Sl 1, k11.
Row 10: Bind off 4 sts, k7, p2tog. (8 sts)
Rep Rows 1–10 for pat.

Pattern Note

Charts for the pattern stitches are included for those preferring to work from charts.

Table Runner

Center Panel

With A, cast on 36 sts.
K1 (selvage st), work Zig Zag Lace to last st, k1 (selvage st).

Working selvage sts as K1 on every row, work 13 reps of Zig Zag Lace.

Bind off purlwise by working Row 1.

Block piece to approx 23½ inches long and 7½ inches wide.

Side Panels

With A, pick up and knit 107 sts inside selvage st along one long edge of center panel.
First 2 rows: Purl 1 row, knit 1 row.
Work Candy Cane Lace once.
Next 2 rows: Purl 1 row, knit 1 row.
Cut yarn, and slip sts to spare needle or piece of waste yarn for holder.
Rep on other side of center panel.

This Christmas table runner uses four different lace patterns and will add a festive touch to any table. Holly berries and leaves provide an optional touch of color.

End Panels

With A, pick up and knit 12 sts along edge of side panel, 34 sts along center panel edge, and 12 sts along other edge of side panel. (58 sts)

Purl one row.

With RS side facing, work Lace Diamond Border once.

Cut yarn, and slip sts to spare needle or waste yarn for holder.

Rep on other end, but do not cut yarn.

Preparing for Edging

Work across 58 sts on needle as follows: k1, pm, k55, pm, k2; pick up and knit 13 sts along edge of end panel as follows: k1, pm, k12; k107 sts from holder; pick up and knit 13 sts along edge of end panel as follows: k11, pm, k2; work across 58 sts on holder at end of table runner as follows: k1, pm, k55, pm, k2; pick up and knit 13 sts along edge of end panel as follows: k1, pm, k12; k107 sts from holder; pick up and knit 13 sts from edge of end panel as follows: k11, pm, k2 along edge of end panel. (382 sts)

Do not join. Cut yarn.

Slip the first st on LH needle to RH needle along with marker to reposition for edging. 3-st corners are indicated by markers. The sts are divided as follows: 55 sts on each end, 130 sts along each side, with 3 sts in each corner.

Edging
Attaching corners of Slant Eyelet Edging:

The Edging is attached as-you-go to the live edge sts of the table runner. To ensure that the edging lies flat at the corners, work corners over the 3 corner stitches between markers as follows: attach Row 2 to first corner st, work Row 4 without attaching to runner (knitting last st), attach Row 6 to 2nd corner st, work Row 8 without attaching, attach Row 10 to last corner stitch. Corner turned.

With B and dpn, cast on 8 sts.

Prep row: Knit.

Work Row 1 of Slant Eyelet Edging.

Starting with Row 2, you will be attaching the edging to the runner (RS facing) by p2tog (last st from edging with 1 st from table runner).

*Work 11 reps, work corner as indicated above, work 26 reps along long edge to next corner, work corner; rep from * until all stitches have been attached and a total of 78 edging reps have been worked.

Cut yarn, leaving a long tail.

Sew ends of edging together using mattress stitch, page 160.

Finishing

Using a tapestry needle, weave yarn ends. Block.

Holly Embellishments
Leaves
Make 8
With C, cast on 5 sts.
  Work 2 rows in St st.
Row 1 (RS): *Inc 1, k1, yo, k1, yo, k1, inc 1. (9 sts)
Rows 2, 4, 6, 10, 12, 16, and 18: Purl.
Row 3: K4, yo, k1, yo, k4. (11 sts)
Row 5: K5, yo, k1, yo, k5. (13 sts)
Row 7: Bind off 3 sts, k2, yo, k1, yo, k6. (12 sts)
Row 8: Bind off 3 sts, p8. (9 sts)

Row 9: Rep Row 3. (11 sts)
Row 11: Rep Row 5. (13 sts)
Row 13: Bind off 3 sts, k9. (10 sts)
Row 14: Bind off 3 sts, p6. (7 sts)
Row 15: Ssk, k3, k2tog. (5 sts)
Row 17: Ssk, k1, k2tog. (3 sts)
Row 19: Sl 1, k2tog, psso. (1 st)
  Fasten off.
  Referring to photo, sew 2 holly leaves to each corner.

Berries
Make 12
With A, cast on 1 st.

Knit in front, back, front, back and front again of st (5 sts made in one st). Turn.
Rows 1 and 3: Knit.
Row 2: Purl.
Row 4: P2tog, p1, p2tog. (3 sts)
Row 5: Knit.
Row 6: P3tog, fasten off.
  Sew 3 berries to each corner, following photo. ✍

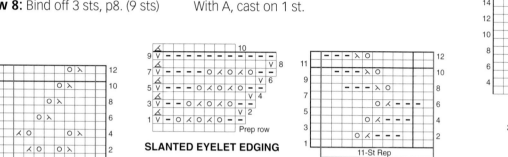

CANDY CANE LACE CHART

STITCH KEY
☐ K on RS, p on WS
⊼ K2tog
⋋ Ssk
◯ Yo

SLANTED EYELET EDGING

STITCH KEY
☐ K on RS, p on WS
— P on RS, k on WS
⊼ K2tog
◯ Yo
∨ Slip 1
⊿ P2tog (1 st edging, 1 st runner)

ZIG ZAG LACE

STITCH KEY
☐ K on RS, p on WS
— P on RS, k on WS
⊼ K2tog
⋋ Ssk
◯ Yo

LACE DIAMOND BORDER

STITCH KEY
☐ K on RS, p on WS
⊼ K2tog
⋋ Ssk
◯ Yo
⊏⊐ Yo, k3, pass 3rd st on RH needle over first 2 sts

DESIGN BY SARA LOUISE HARPER

Think Warm Thoughts

Finished Size

Approx 8 x 70 inches, excluding Fringe

Materials

- Plymouth Outback Mohair 70 percent mohair/26 percent wool/4 percent nylon bulky weight yarn (218 yds/100g per skein): 1 skein #858
- Size 10½ (6.5mm) needles or size needed to obtain gauge
- Medium size crochet hook for attaching fringe

Gauge

11 sts and 14 rows = 4 inches/ 10cm in pat st
To save time, take time to check gauge.

Special Abbreviation

yo2 (double yarn-over): Bring yarn forward, then around needle and forward again, making 2 yarn-overs. On following WS row, k1, p1 into the first loop and drop the second.

Pattern Stitch

Leaning Ladders
(multiple of 9 sts + 4)

Rows 1, 3, 5, 7, 9: *Ssk, yo2, [k2tog] twice, k3, yo; rep from * to last 4 sts, ssk, yo2, k2tog.

Row 2 (and all WS rows): Purl across, working k1, p1 into yo2 loops.

Row 11: *Ssk, yo2, k2tog, k5; rep from * to last 4 sts, ssk, yo2, k2tog.

Rows 13, 15, 17, 19, 21: *Ssk, yo2, k2tog, yo, k3, ssk; rep from * to last 4 sts, ssk, yo2, k2tog.

Row 23: Rep Row 11.

Row 24: Rep Row 2.
Rep Rows 1–24 for pat.

Pattern Note

A chart for the pattern stitch is included for those preferring to work from a chart.

Scarf

Cast on 22 sts.
Purl 1 row.
Work Leaning Ladders pat 10 times, or until scarf measures desired length, ending last rep with Row 23.
Loosely bind off all sts, working k1, p1 in yo2 loops.
Block gently, stretching very slightly to enhance lace pattern.

Fringe

Following Fringe instructions on page 161, make Single Knot fringe.
Cut 60 lengths of yarn, each approx 18 inches long. Holding 6 strands per fringe and using a crochet hook, attach 5 evenly-spaced fringes to each end of scarf. Trim ends evenly. ꙳

		−									−					Row 23
⊼	o	o	⊼					⊼	o	o	⊼					
		−									−					
⊼	o	o	⊼	⊼			⊼	o	⊼	o	o	⊼				Rows 13, 15, 17, 19, 21
		−									−					
⊼	o	o	⊼	⊼				⊼	⊼	o	o	⊼				Row 11
		−									−					
⊼	o	o	⊼	o				⊼	⊼	o	o	⊼				Rows 1, 3, 5, 7, 9

9-St Rep

LEANING LADDERS CHART

STITCH KEY	
□	K on RS, p on WS
⊼	K2tog
⊼	Ssk
o	Yo
o o	Yo2
−	K1, p1 in yo2 loop

*This wonderfully soft mohair
scarf knits up quickly for use as
a gift—maybe for yourself!*

DESIGN BY CELESTE PINHEIRO

Dance Around The Tree

Finished Size

INTERMEDIATE

Approx 52 inches diameter

Materials

5 BULKY

- Plymouth Encore Chunky 75 percent acrylic/25 percent wool bulky weight yarn (143 yds/100g per ball): 8 skeins soft white #146 (MC); 1 skein each brown heather #1444 (A), quiet red #9601 (B), oatmeal heather #240(C), fir heather #670 (D) and pink #29 (E) (or small amount)
- Size 10 (6.0mm) needles or size needed to obtain gauge
- Size 10½ (6.5mm) needles
- Stitch holders
- Tapestry needle
- 8 (1-inch) buttons

Gauge

14 sts and 18 rows = 4 inches/10 cm in St st using smaller needles To save time, take time to check gauge.

Pattern Stitch

Fair Isle Pattern (6-st repeat) See Chart on page 148.

Pattern Note

The first and last stitches of each section are selvage sts. Work these sts in St st in the dominant color of the row.

Tree Skirt

Section
Make 3
With larger needles and MC, cast on 146 sts.

Work 6 rows in St st, ending with a WS row.

Next 4 rows: With B, knit.

Next row (RS): K1 (selvage st), work Fair Isle pat to last st, k1 (selvage st). *See Pattern Note.*

Next 4 rows: Complete Chart. Cut B.

Next row (WS): Change to smaller needles, and purl with MC.

Dec row (RS): K1 (selvage st), *K46, k2tog; rep from * twice

more, end k1 (selvage st). (143 sts)

Rep last 2 rows, working 1 less st sts before dec on each succeeding Dec row, until 26 sts rem.

Place sts on holder.

Make 2 more sections, leaving sts of 3rd section on needle.

Join sections

Slip sts of the 2 sections on holders to needle. (78 sts)

While Sugar Plum Fairies danced in their heads, Santa and his reindeer danced below the tree ...

Next row (WS): K24, ssk, k2tog, k22, ssk, k2tog, knit to end. (74 sts)
Next row: K1, *k2tog, yo; rep from * to last 3 sts, k1, yo, k2.
Next row: Knit.
 Bind off.

Assembly
Sew sections together, leaving one seam open for buttonband.

Buttonband
With RS facing, using smaller needles and MC, pick up and knit 85 sts evenly along left edge.
 Knit 7 rows.
 Bind off.

Buttonhole band
With RS facing, using smaller needles and MC, pick up and knit 85 sts evenly along right edge.
 Knit 3 rows.
Buttonhole row (RS): K3, *bind off 2, k9; rep from * 6 more times, bind off 2, k3.
Next row: Knit, casting on 2 sts over bound-off sts on previous row.
 Knit 2 rows.
 Bind off.
 Sew buttons opposite buttonholes.
 Cut 6 strands from different colors about 72 inches long. Braid for tie, tying overhand knots at ends. Thread tie through eyelets at center.

Appliqués
Make 1 santa, 4 reindeer, and 4 trees (see Ornaments/ Appliqués under Dashing Ornaments beg on page 152).
 Referring to photo sew to tree skirt.

FAIR ISLE CHART

STITCH & COLOR KEY
☐ Soft white (MC)
■ Quiet red (B)
◉ Make bobble (K1, p1, k1, p1 in same st, turn, k2, turn, p4, turn, pull first 3 sts over last st)

PERFECT GIFT PURSE CONTINUED FROM PAGE 130

time. When desired sizes have been reached, remove the pieces and rinse under lukewarm water. Roll in towel to remove excess water.
 Gently pull base of purse to oval shape. Pull handle to about the same width as base. A small towel can be placed inside the base to maintain the oval shape. Pin the pocket out on a dry towel, forming a rectangle about 4¼ x 5 inches.

Dry away from the sun, checking the shaping periodically. It may take several days for the pieces to dry completely.
 When both pieces are dry, turn purse wrong side out. Pin pocket in desired location on one side.
 Using sharp needle and heavy sewing thread, whipstitch in place.
 Turn right side out, and brush the mohair bands with a stiff bristle brush.

SOCKS WITH A TWINKLE CONTINUED FROM PAGE 132

Shape Star Toe
Rnd 1: N1: *Knit to last 2 sts, k2tog; rep from * on each of the 3 rem needles. (56 sts)
Rnd 2: Knit.
Rep [Rnds 1 and 2] 7 times. (28 sts)

Rep Rnd 1 until 8 sts rem.
 Break yarn, leaving an 8-inch tail.
 Using a tapestry needle, pull yarn through the rem sts and pull closed.

DESIGN BY CELESTE PINHEIRO

Waiting For Santa

Materials

INTERMEDIATE

- Plymouth Encore Worsted 75 percent acrylic/25 percent wool medium weight yarn (200 yds/100g per skein): 1 skein each soft white #146 (MC), brown heather #1444 (A), quiet red #9601 (B), oatmeal heather #240 (C), fir heather #670 (D), pink #29 (E) or small amount
- Size 6 (4mm) needles
- Size 8 (5mm) straight and double-pointed needles or size needed to obtain gauge
- Stitch holder
- Tapestry needle

Gauge

16 sts and 22 rows = 4 inches/ 10cm in St st with larger needles
To save time, take time to check gauge.

Special Abbreviations

N1, N2, N3: Needle 1, needle 2, needle 3

Stitch Patterns

Fair Isle Pattern (6-st repeat)
See Chart on page 151.

Stripe Sequence

*Work 6 rows in St st MC, 4 rnds D; rep from * twice more, end knit 6 rnds MC.

Pattern Notes

The leg is worked back and forth; the foot is worked in the round.
   The first and last sts of leg are

Make a unique
stocking for
each member
of the family,
putting different
appliqués on
each one.

selvage sts and are worked in St st. They will be eliminated before working the heel.

Stocking

With smaller needles and MC, cast on 62 sts.

First 11 rows: Work in St st, ending with a WS row.

Next 4 rows: With A, knit.

Next row (RS): Change to larger needles and k1 (selvage), work Fair Isle chart to last st, k1 (selvage st).

Maintaining first and last sts in St st, complete Fair Isle chart.

With MC, work even in St st until piece measures 13 inches from beg, ending with a WS row.

Heel flap

With RS facing, sl 16, place next 30 sts on holder, sl 16. (32 sts)

Row 1 (RS): With B, k2tog, knit to last 2 sts, ssk.

Continue in St st for 17 more rows.

Turn heel

Row 1 (RS): K16, ssk, k1, turn.

Row 2: Sl 1, p3, p2tog, p1, turn.

Row 3: Sl 1, k4, ssk, k1, turn.

Row 4: Sl 1, p5, p2tog, p1, turn.

Row 5: Sl 1, k6, ssk, k1, turn.

Rows 6-13: Continue in this manner, working 1 more st each row before dec.

Row 14: Sl 1, p14, p2tog. (16 sts)

Cut B.

Gusset and foot

Pick-up rnd: With dpn (N1), sl 8 sts, then with MC, k8, pick up and knit 12 sts along left side of heel; with N2, k30 from holder; with N3, pick up and knit 12 sts along right side of heel, knit the 8 slipped sts on N1. Join.

Note: _The beg of rnd is now in middle of heel._ (70 sts arranged N1:20 sts; N2: 30 sts; N3: 20 sts)

Rnd 1: Knit.

Rnd 2: N1: Knit to last 2 sts, k2tog; N2: knit; N3: ssk, knit to end.

Rep [Rnds 1 and 2] 4 more times. (60 sts)

At the same time, work Stripe sequence, starting from Pick-up rnd.

Work even until Stripe sequence is complete.

Toe

Rnd 1: With B, knit 1 rnd.

Rnd 2: N1: K to last 2 sts, k2tog; N2: ssk, to last 2 sts, k2tog; N3: ssk, k to end of rnd. (56 sts)

Rep Rnds 1 and 2 until 16 sts rem.

Next rnd: K2tog around. (8 sts)

Break off yarn, leaving a 6 inch tail. With tapestry needle, draw tail through rem sts 2 times and pull tight.

Assembly

Make appliqués as desired (see Ornaments and Appliqués pattern) and sew on leg.

Sew leg seam.

Hanger

Cut 2 (8-inch) lengths of MC, B and D. Braid, leaving decorative tails at each end. Join in loop with overhand knot. Attach to top back of sock.

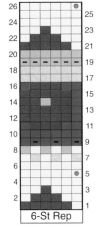

STITCH & COLOR KEY
- ☐ Soft white (MC)
- ▨ Brown heather (A)
- ■ Quiet red (B)
- ▥ Oatmeal heather (C)
- ■ Moss (D)
- – P on RS, using color indicated
- ● Make bobble: (K1, p1, k1, p1 in same st, turn, p4, turn, pull first 3 sts over last st)

6-St Rep

FAIR ISLE CHART

Dashing Ornaments

DESIGN BY CELESTE PINHEIRO

Finished Sizes

INTERMEDIATE

Reindeer: Approx 8 inches long
Santa: Approx 8 inches long
Tree: Approx 8 x 5½ inches

Materials

4 MEDIUM
5 BULKY

- Plymouth Encore Worsted 75 percent acrylic/25 percent wool medium weight yarn (200 yds/100g per skein): 1 skein each soft white #146 (MC), brown heather #1444 (A), quiet red #9601 (B), oatmeal heather #240 (C), fir heather #670 (D); small amount pink #29 (E)
- Plymouth Encore Chunky 75 percent acrylic/25 percent wool bulky weight yarn (143 yds/100g per ball): 1 skein each soft white #146 (MC), brown heather #1444 (A), quiet red #9601 (B), oatmeal heather #240(C), fir heather #670 (D); small amount pink #29 (E)
- Size 8 (5mm) double-pointed needles or size needed to obtain gauge
- Size 10 (6mm) double-pointed needles or size needed to obtain gauge
- Small crochet hook for Santa's fringe beard
- Tapestry needle

Gauges

14 sts and 19 rows = 4 inches/ 10cm in St st with larger needles and Encore Chunky
16 sts and 22 rows = 4 inches/ 10cm in St st with smaller needles and Encore Worsted

To save time, take time to check gauge.

Special Abbreviations

I-cord: With dpn and yarn indicated, leaving a 6-inch tail, cast on number of sts indicated. *Knit all sts, do not turn. Slip sts from RH needle back to LH needle. Rep from * as instructed. Break yarn, leaving a 6-inch tail. Use tapestry needle to draw tail through the rem sts. Finish by drawing tails through center of cord, then cut.

M1 (Make 1): Insert tip of LH needle under horizontal strand between st just worked and next st and knit through back loop.

MB (Make Bobble): (k1, p1, k1, p1) into next st, turn; k4, turn; purl, turn; pull first 3 sts over last st.

Pattern Notes

Directions are the same for Chunky or Worsted yarn. Use Chunky for Tree Skirt appliqués and Worsted for Stocking appliqués. Use either for Ornaments.

Backs are omitted for appliqués.

Ornaments/Appliqués
Reindeer
Arms
Make 1
With A, cast on 4 sts, and work 2 rows of I-cord.

Change to C, and work 25 rows of I-cord.

Change to A, and work 3 rows

Trim your tree with these whimsical knitted ornaments.

of I-cord. Finish as instructed in Special Abbreviations.

Legs
Make 2
With A, cast on 4 sts, and work 2 rows of I-cord.

Change to C, and work 15 more rows of I-cord; place on holder.

Leave sts for 2nd leg on needle.

Body Front
Slip sts for first leg to needle. (8 sts)

With C, purl across.

Next row (RS): *K2, M1; rep from * twice more, end k2. (11 sts)

Work 3 rows in St st.

Next (Dec) row: K1, k2tog, work to last 3 sts, ssk, k1.

Continue in St st and work Dec row [every 4th row] once, then [every other row] once. (5 sts)

Work 7 rows even in St st.

Bind off.

Body Back
With C, cast on 8 sts.

Purl 1 row.

Next row (RS): *K2, M1; rep from * twice more, end k2. (11 sts)

Next row: Purl.

Next row (RS): K5, MB, k5.

Next row: Purl.

Continue as for front, beg with Dec row.

Head
Note: *Head is worked from top down.*
With C, cast on 14 sts.

Beg with a WS row, work 3 rows in St st.

Next (Dec) row: K2tog, work to last 2 sts, ssk.

Continue in St st and work Dec row [every other row] twice more. (8 sts)

Work 5 rows even in St st.

Next row (RS): K2tog across. (4 sts)

Next row: Purl.

Next row: K2tog twice. (2 sts)

Next row: P2tog. Fasten off.

Assembly
Sew back to front, but stop seam just before last side dec.

At this point, stuff belly with a bit of waste yarn and sandwich arms between front and back. Finish sewing body.

Ears
Pinch top corner of head on each side about ½ inch in from corner, wrap yarn around and tie.

Face
With A, make 2 French Knot eyes, page 163. With A or B, make French Knot nose.

Antlers (ornament version)
With A, cast on 3 sts. Work 7 rows of I-cord, and finish as instructed above.

Sew to top of head.

Antlers (appliqué version)
With A, create antlers in chain st, page 163, on main fabric.

Sew head to top of body.

Santa
Arms
Make 1
With E, cast on 4 sts, and knit 3 rows of I-cord.

Change to MC, and knit 1 row of I-cord, then purl 2 rows of I-cord.

Change to B, and knit 25 rows of I-cord.

Change to MC, knit 1 row of I-cord, then purl 2 rows of I-cord.

Change to E, and knit 3 rows of I-cord.

Bind off.

Legs
Make 2
WIth A, cast on 4 sts, knit 6 rows of I-cord.

Change to B, knit 15 rows of I-cord.

Bind off.

Coat, head and hat
Make 1 for appliqué, 2 for ornament
With MC, cast on 13 sts. Knit 3 rows.

Next 2 rows: With B, knit 1 row, purl 1 row.

Dec row: K1, k2tog, knit to last 3 sts, ssk, k1.

Continue in St st and work Dec row [every 4th row] once, then [every other row] once, ending on a WS row. (7 sts)

Next 2 rows: With MC, knit.

Next 6 rows: With E, work in St st.

Next 4 rows: With MC, knit.
Next 2 rows: With B, work in St st.
Dec row (front and appliqué):
K1, k2tog, knit to end.
or
Dec row (back): Knit to last 3 sts,
ssk, k1.
   Continuing in St st, work Dec
row (front or back) [every 4th row]
3 times more. (3 sts)
Next row: K3 tog. Bind off.

Assembly
Sew front and back together,
sandwiching arms near top of red
"suit".
   With A, work duplicate st eyes,
page 162.
   With E, make French Knot nose,
page 163.
   With B, work duplicate st mouth.
   With MC and crochet hook,
make and attach 3 short pieces of
fringe in garter st ridge for beard,
page 156.
   With A, make 2 French Knot
buttons on "suit".
   Attach legs to "neck" under coat.

Tree
**Make 2 for ornament, 1 for
appliqué**
*Note: First and last sts of "tree"
are selvage sts.*

Trunk
With A, cast on 5 sts. Knit 9 rows.

Tree
With D, cast on 11 sts, knit across 5
"trunk" sts, cast on 11 sts. (27 sts)
Next 3 rows: Beg with a WS row,
work 3 rows St st.
Dec row: K1, k2tog, knit to last 3
sts, ssk, k1. (25 sts)
   Continuing in St st, work Dec row
[every other row] 6 more times,
ending with a RS row. (13 sts)
   Cast on 5 sts at end of row just
worked.
Next row (WS): Purl to end, cast
on 5 sts. (23 sts)
Next 4 rows: Work in St st.
   Work Dec row [every other
row] 9 times, ending with a WS
row. (5 sts)
Next row: K1, sk2p, k1. (3 sts)
Next row: Bind off.

Assembly
With B, make random French
Knots for "ornament
balls".
   With MC,
embroider random
"stars" as in photo.
   Sew front and back
together.

Hanger
Make 1 for each ornament
Cut 3 (9-inch) lengths of MC, B
and D.
   Knot together at one end,
leaving decorative
tails.
   Braid, then
knot end, leaving
decorative tails.
   Make loop by
knotting ends
together.
   Attach to top of
ornament. ✍

GENERAL INFORMATION

BASIC STITCHES

Garter Stitch
On straight needles, knit every row. When working in the round on circular or double-pointed needles, knit one round then purl one round.

Stockinette Stitch
On straight needles, knit right-side rows and purl wrong-side rows. When working in the round on circular or double-pointed needles, knit all rounds.

Reverse Stockinette Stitch
On straight needles, purl right-side rows and knit wrong-side rows. When working in the round on circular or double-pointed needles, purl all rounds.

Ribbing
Ribbing combines knit and purl stitches within a row to give stretch to the garment. Ribbing is most often used for the lower edge of the front and back, the cuffs and neck edge of garments.

The rib pattern is established on the first row. On subsequent rows the knit stitches are knitted and purl stitches are purled to form the ribs.

READING PATTERN INSTRUCTIONS
Before beginning a pattern, read through it to make sure you are familiar with the abbreviations that are used.

Some patterns may be written for more than one size. In this case the smallest size is given first, and others are placed in parentheses. When only one number is given, it applies to all sizes.

You may wish to highlight the numbers for the size you are making before beginning. It is also helpful to place a self-adhesive sheet on the pattern to note any changes made while working the pattern.

MEASURING
To measure pieces, lay them flat on a smooth surface. Take the measurement in the middle of the piece. For example, measure the length to the armhole in the center of the front or back piece, not along the outer edge where the edges tend to curve or roll.

GAUGE
The single most important factor in determining the finished size of a knit item is the gauge. Although not as important for flat, one-piece items, it is important when making a clothing item that needs to fit properly.

It is important to make a stitch gauge swatch about 4 inches square with recommended patterns and needles before beginning.

Measure the swatch. If the number of stitches and rows are fewer than indicated under "Gauge" in the pattern, your needles are too large. Try another swatch with smaller-size needles. If the number of stitches and rows are more than indicated under "Gauge" in the pattern, your needles are too small. Try another swatch with larger-size needles.

Continue to adjust needles until correct gauge is achieved.

WORKING FROM CHARTS
When working with more than one color in a row, sometimes a chart is provided to help follow the pattern. On the chart each square represents one stitch. A key is given indicating the color or stitch represented by each color or symbol in the box.

When working in rows, odd-numbered rows are usually read from right to left and even-numbered rows from left to right.

For color-work charts, rows beginning at the right represent the right side of the work and are usually knit. Rows beginning at the left represent the wrong side and are usually purled.

When working in rounds, every row on the chart is a right-side row, and is read from right to left.

USE OF ZERO
In patterns that include various sizes, zeros are sometimes necessary. For example, k0 (0,1) means if you are making the smallest or middle size, you would do nothing, and if you are making the largest size, you would k1.

GLOSSARY

bind off—used to finish an edge

cast on—process of making foundation stitches used in knitting

decrease—means of reducing the number of stitches in a row

increase—means of adding to the number of stitches in a row

intarsia—method of knitting a multicolored pattern into the fabric

knitwise—insert needle into stitch as if to knit

make 1—method of increasing using the strand between the last stitch worked and the next stitch

place marker—placing a purchased marker or loop of

contrasting yarn onto the needle for ease in working a pattern repeat

purlwise—insert needle into stitch as if to purl

right side—side of garment or piece that will be seen when worn

selvage (selvedge) stitch—edge stitch used to make seaming easier

slip, slip, knit—method of decreasing by moving stitches from left needle to right needle and working them together

slip stitch—an unworked stitch slipped from left needle to right needle, usually as if to purl

wrong side—side that will be

inside when garment is worn

work even—continue to work in the pattern as established without working any increases or decreases

work in pattern as established—continue to work following the pattern stitch as it has been set up or established on the needle, working any increases or decreases in such a way that the established pattern remains the same

yarn over—method of increasing by wrapping the yarn over the right needle without working a stitch

Skill Levels

■□□□
BEGINNER

Projects for first-time knitters using basic knit and purl stitches. Minimal shaping.

■■□□
EASY

Projects using basic stitches, repetitive stitch patterns, simple color changes and simple shaping and finishing.

■■■□
INTERMEDIATE

Projects with a variety of stitches, such as basic cables and lace, simple intarsia, double-pointed needles and knitting in the round needle techniques, mid-level shaping and finishing.

■■■■
EXPERIENCED

Projects using advanced techniques and stitches, such as short rows, Fair Isle, more intricate intarsia, cables, lace patterns and numerous color changes.

Standard Abbreviations

[ ] work instructions within brackets as many times as directed

( ) work instructions within parentheses in the place directed

** repeat instructions between the asterisks as directed

* repeat instructions following the single asterisk as directed

approx approximately

beg begin/beginning

CC contrasting color

ch chain stitch

cm centimeter(s)

cn cable needle

dec decrease/decreases/decreasing

dpn(s) double-pointed needle(s)

g gram

inc increase/increases/increasing

k knit

k2tog knit 2 stitches together

LH left hand

lp(s) loop(s)

m meter(s)

M1 make one stitch

MC main color

mm millimeter(s)

oz ounce(s)

p purl

pat(s) pattern(s)

p2tog purl 2 stitches together

psso pass slipped stitch over

rem remain/remaining

rep repeat(s)

rev St st reverse stockinette stitch

RH right hand

rnd(s) rounds

RS right side

skp slip, knit, pass stitch over—one stitch decreased

sk2p slip 1, knit 2

together, pass slip stitch over the knit 2 together; 2 stitches have been decreased

sl slip

sl 1k slip 1 knitwise

sl 1p slip 1 purlwise

sl st slip stitch(es)

ssk slip, slip, knit these 2 stitches together—a decrease

ssp slip, slip, purl these 2 stitches together through the back loops [or tbl]—a decrease

st(s) stitch(es)

St st stockinette stitch/stocking stitch

tbl through back loop(s)

tog together

WS wrong side

wyib with yarn in back

wyif with yarn in front

yd(s) yard(s)

yfwd yarn forward

yo yarn over

Stranded or Fair Isle Knitting (2-Colors)

Changing colors of yarn within the row is called Stranded or Fair Isle knitting. This type of knitting can be worked either with both yarns in one hand or with one yarn in each hand. Carry the yarns along the wrong side of the fabric, working each color in the order indicated by the pattern. One color should always be carried under the other, whether you are knitting or purling—the strands will run parallel on the wrong side. They should never change positions; if they do, it will be apparent on the right side of the fabric. Carry both yarns to the end of each row and "lock" them in position on the last stitch.

Photo A

When one of the yarns is carried across the back for more than 5 stitches (or about an inch), the yarn should be caught into the back of one of the stitches that is worked with the other yarn. This will prevent snags caused by long floats.

Fair Isle knitting creates a denser fabric than plain Stockinette knitting. Always work your gauge swatch in pattern before beginning your project. Watch your tension, ensuring that the stranded yarn is not pulled too tight; this will create puckers on the front of the fabric.

Photo B

Intarsia

In certain patterns there are larger areas of color within the piece. Since this type of pattern requires a new color only for that section, it is not necessary to carry the yarn back and forth across the back. For this type of color change, a separate ball of yarn or bobbin is used for each color, making the yarn available only where needed. Bring the new yarn being used up-and-around the yarn just worked; this will "lock" the colors and prevent holes from occurring at the join.

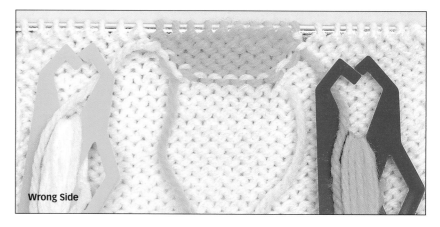

Wrong Side

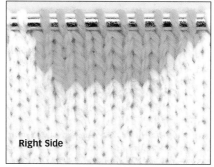

Right Side

Cables

Cable needles are used to hold stitches either in front or in back of the work and out of the way while other stitches are worked. They are made with a point at both ends so stitches can be slipped on at one end and worked off at the other. Some cable needles have a curved area in the middle to hold the stitches so they won't slip off.

Twisting the Cable

A cable can be twisted with any number of stitches. The following illustrates a cable worked over six stitches. Half of the stitches are held behind the work on a cable needle while the other stitches are being worked. Then the stitches on the cable needle are worked. This changes the order of the stitches and forms a cable.

Slip next three stitches onto cable needle and hold in back of work. (Photo A) Knit next three stitches from left-hand needle. Knit three stitches from cable needle to complete the cable twist.

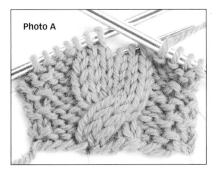
Photo A

Twisting the cable by holding the stitches in the back each time creates a cable that twists to the right. (Photo B)

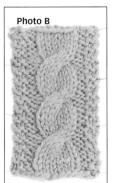
Photo B

To twist the cable to the left, slip the next three stitches onto a cable needle and hold the stitches in front of the work. (Photo C) Knit the next three stitches. Knit the stitches from the cable needle to complete the cable twist.

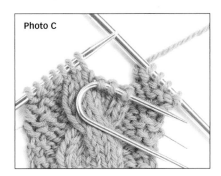
Photo C

Holding the stitches in the front each time results in a cable that twists to the left. (Photo D)

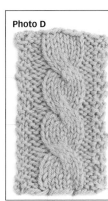
Photo D

Zipper How-To

Zippers can easily be added to a knit garment. Different weights of garments need different-weight zippers. Heavy separating zippers are used on jackets and cardigans, while regular dressmaking zippers are used for neck or skirt openings.

The zipper should be sewn in by hand using a backstitch through both the zipper and knit piece.

To add a zipper, place the knit edges over the zipper so the zipper teeth are covered and the seam is centered over the zipper. From the right side, pin in place.

On the wrong side, tack the edges of the zipper to the garment. Turn to the right side and backstitch the zipper in place.

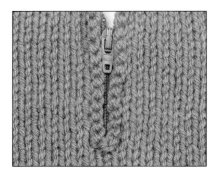
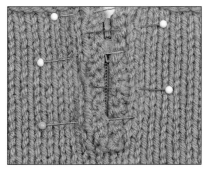
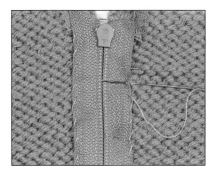

Seam Finishes

Mattress Seam

This type of seam can be used for vertical seams (like side seams). It is worked with the right sides of the pieces facing you, making it easier to match stitches for stripe patterns. It is worked between the first and second stitch at the edge of the piece and works best when the first stitch is a selvage stitch.

To work this seam, thread a tapestry needle with matching yarn. Insert the needle into one corner of work from back to front, just above the cast-on stitch, leaving a 3-inch tail. Take needle to edge of other piece and bring it from back to front at the corner of this piece.

Return to the first piece and insert the needle from the right to wrong side where the thread comes out of the piece. Slip the needle upward under two horizontal threads and bring the needle through to the right side.

Cross to the other side and repeat the same process "down where you came out, under two threads and up."

Continue working back and forth on the two pieces in the same manner for about an inch, then gently pull on the thread pulling the two pieces together. (Photo A)

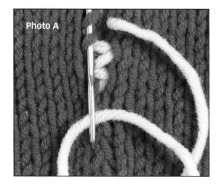
Photo A

Complete the seam and fasten off. Use the beginning tail to even-up the lower edge by working a figure 8 between the cast-on stitches at the corners. Insert the threaded needle from front to back under both threads of the corner cast-on stitch on the edge opposite the tail, then into the same stitch on the first edge. Pull gently until the figure 8 fills the gap. (Photo B)

Photo B

When a project is made with a textured yarn that will not pull easily through the pieces, it is recommended that a smooth yarn of the same color be used to work the seam.

Garter Stitch Seams

The "bumps" of the garter stitch selvage nestle between each other in a garter stitch seam, often producing a nearly reversible seam. This is a good seam for afghan strips and blocks of the same color. Starting as for the mattress seam, work from bump to bump, alternating sides. In this case you enter each stitch only once.

Matching Patterns

When it comes to matching stripes and other elements in a sweater design, a simple formula makes things line up perfectly:

Begin the seam in the usual way.

Enter the first stitch of each new color stripe (or pattern detail) on the same side as you began the seam; i.e. the same side as your tail is hanging.

3-Needle Bind Off

Use this technique for seaming two edges together, such as when joining a shoulder seam. Hold the live edge stitches on two separate needles with right sides together.

With a third needle, knit together a stitch from the front needle with one from the back.

Repeat, knitting a stitch from the front needle with one from the back needle once more.

Slip the first stitch over the second.

Repeat knitting, a front and back pair of stitches together, then bind one pair off.

Pompoms

Cut two cardboard circles in size specified in pattern. Cut a hole in the center of each circle, about ½ inch in diameter. Thread a tapestry needle with a length of yarn doubled. Holding both circles together, insert needle through center hole, over the outside edge, and through center again (Fig. 1) until entire circle is covered and center hole is filled (thread more length of yarn as needed).

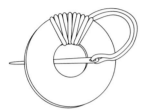

Fig. 1

With sharp scissors, cut yarn between the two circles all around the circumference. (Fig. 2)

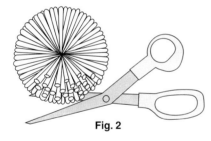

Fig. 2

Using two 12-inch strands of yarn, slip yarn between circles and overlap yarn ends 2 or 3 times (Fig. 3) to prevent knot from slipping, pull tightly and tie into a firm knot.

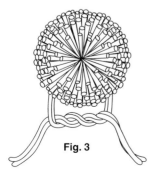

Fig. 3

Remove cardboard and fluff out pompom by rolling it between your hands. Trim even with scissors; leave the tying ends for when attaching pompom to project.

Fringe

Cut a piece of cardboard half as long as fringe length specified in instructions plus ½ inch for trimming. Wind yarn loosely and evenly around cardboard. When cardboard is filled, cut yarn across one end. Do this several times then begin fringing. Wind additional strands as necessary.

SINGLE KNOT FRINGE

Hold specified number of strands for one knot together, fold in half. Hold project to be fringed with right side facing you. Use crochet hook to draw folded end through space or stitch indicated from right to wrong side.

Pull loose ends through folded section.

Draw knot up firmly. Space knots as indicated in pattern instructions.

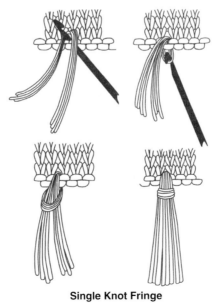

Single Knot Fringe

Kitchener Stitch

This method of weaving with two needles is used for the toes of socks and flat seams. To weave the edges together and form an unbroken line of stockinette stitch, divide all stitches evenly onto two knitting needles—one behind the other. Thread yarn into tapestry needle. Hold needles with wrong sides together and work from right to left as follows:

Step 1: Insert tapestry needle into first stitch on front needle as to purl. Draw yarn through stitch, leaving stitch on knitting needle.

Step 2: Insert tapestry needle into the first stitch on the back needle as to purl. Draw yarn through stitch and slip stitch off knitting needle.

Step 3: Insert tapestry needle into the next stitch on same (back) needle as to knit, leaving stitch on knitting needle.

Step 4: Insert tapestry needle into the first stitch on the front needle as to knit. Draw yarn through stitch and slip stitch off knitting needle.

Step 5: Insert tapestry needle into the next stitch on same (front) needle as to purl. Draw yarn through stitch, leaving stitch on knitting needle.

Repeat Steps 2 through 5 until one stitch is left on each needle. Then repeat Steps 2 and 4. Fasten off. Woven stitches should be the same size as adjacent knitted stitches.

Duplicate Stitch

As the name suggests, duplicate stitch imitates the knitted stitch, but it is actually embroidery worked on the surface of the knitted fabric. It's frequently used to add color details, such as a stripe or small motif, but you can also use it to correct small mistakes. Knit Tip: Remember that this new stitch sits on top or covers an existing stitch. Adjust your tension carefully.

3. Complete the stitch by returning the needle to where you began.

1. Bring yarn to the outside at the base of the stitch below the stitch to be duplicated.

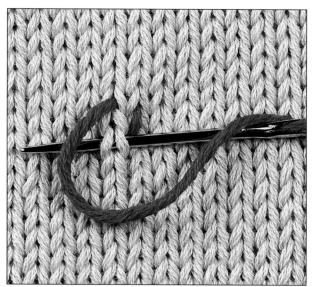

4. When working a series of horizontal duplicate stitches, complete one stitch and begin the adjacent stitch in one step.

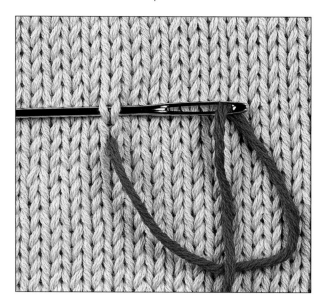

2. Pull yarn through to front. Place needle from right to left behind both sides of the stitch above the one being duplicated.

Embroidery Stitches

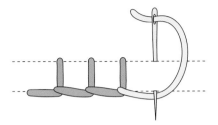

Buttonhole Stitch

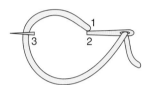  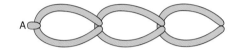

Chain Stitch

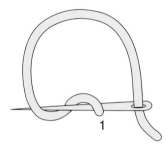 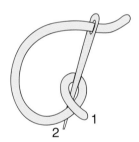

French Knot

Twisted Cord

Items sometimes require a cord as a drawstring closing or strap. The number of lengths and weight of the yarn determines the thickness of the cord.

To form the cord, hold the number of strands of yarn indicated together matching the ends. Attach one end to a doorknob or hook. Twist the other end in one direction until the length is tightly twisted and begins to kink.

Sometimes the lengths are folded in half before twisting. In this case the loose ends are attached to the

doorknob and a pencil is slipped into the folded loop at the other end. Turn the pencil to twist the cord.

Once the cord is tightly twisted, continue to hold the twisted end while folding the yarn in the middle. Remove the end from the knob or hook and match the two ends, then release them allowing the cord to twist on itself.

Trim the cord ends to the desired length and knot each end. If the cord is woven through eyelets, it may be necessary to tie a second knot in the end to prevent it from slipping back through the eyelet opening.

Felting Instructions

The Felt Formula

Felting is not a precise science. Wool felts when exposed to water, heat, and agitation, but each element is hard to control precisely. As a result, each individual project may vary in the way it felts.

Felting can be done in the sink, but washing machines get the job done more quickly. Each washing machine is different, and the amount your machine felts a piece after one cycle may vary from your neighbors'. So be sure to follow the specific felting instructions of the piece you are making, and check your piece several times during the felting process to make sure you are getting the desired results.

The felting process releases fibers which can clog your washing machine. Therefore, you may want to place items in a roomy mesh bag before putting them in the washing machine. Also, adding other laundry, such as jeans, when felting will increase the amount of agitation and speed up the process. Be careful not to use items that shed fibers of their own, such as towels.

Felting Facts

Felting a knit or crochet piece makes it shrink. Therefore, the piece you knit must start out much larger than the finished felted size will be. Shrinkage varies since there are so many factors that affect it. These variables include water temperature, the hardness of the water, how much (and how long) the piece is agitated, the amount and type of soap used, yarn brand, fiber content and color.

You can control how much your piece felts by watching it closely. Check your piece after about 10 minutes to see how quickly it is felting. Look at the stitch definition and size to determine if the piece has been felted enough.

How to Felt

Place items to be felted in the washing machine along with one tablespoon of dish detergent and a pair of jeans or other laundry. (Remember, do not felt projects with other clothing that release their own fibers.) Set washing machine on smallest load and use hot water. Start machine and check progress after ten minutes. Check progress more frequently after piece starts to felt. Reset the machine if needed to continue the agitation cycle. Do not allow machine to drain and spin until the piece is the desired size. As the piece becomes more felted, you may need to pull it into shape.

When the piece has felted to the desired size, rinse it by hand in warm water. Remove the excess water either by rolling in a towel and squeezing, or in the spin cycle of your washing machine.

Block the piece into shape, and let air dry. Do not dry in clothes dryer. For pieces that need to conform to a particular shape (such as a hat or purse), stuff the piece with a towel to help it hold its shape while drying. Felted items are very strong, so don't be afraid to push and pull it into the desired shape. It may take several hours or several days for the pieces to dry completely.

After the piece is completely dry excess fuzziness can be trimmed with scissors if a smoother surface is desired, or the piece can be brushed for a fuzzier appearance.

Pick Up and Knit

This technique is often used to add a border or collar to the edge of a knitted piece. You may also use it to work a sleeve from the armhole down to the cuff. It makes a very neat finish with no seaming required. Knit Tip: As the number of stitches per inch is rarely the same as the number of rows per inch in Stockinette stitch, you will usually pick up approximately 3 stitches for every 4 rows. You may wish to check this on a swatch.

3. Pull loop through to front.

1. With right side facing, working one stitch in from edge, insert tip of needle in space between first and second stitch.

4. Repeat steps 1 through 3.

2. Wrap yarn around needle. (We used a contrasting color, but you will want to use the same yarn you used for your project.)

Short Rows/Wrap

Short rows add length to part of a piece of knitting. For example, the heel of a sock is shaped with short rows. Or instead of binding off the shoulders of a sweater in a series of stair steps, you can work a series of short rows, and then bind off all the stitches at once in a smooth line. This following wrapping technique eliminates the holes that might otherwise occur.

4. To work stitch and wrap together from right side, lift wrap with tip of needle.

1. On a knit row, bring the yarn to the front of work, slip next stitch as if to purl.

5. Insert tip of needle into stitch, knit stitch and wrap together. (Wrap will automatically fall to wrong side of fabric.)

2. Take yarn to back.

3. Turn work, slip first stitch as if to purl (wrap made), complete row.

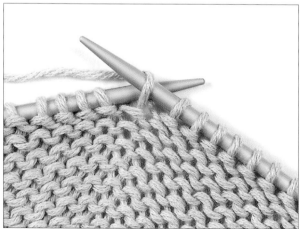

6. On a purl row, take yarn to back of work, slip next stitch as if to purl.

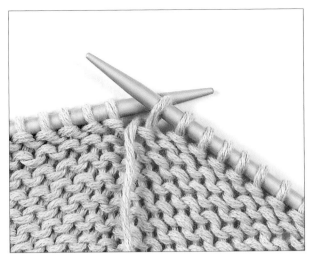

7. Bring yarn to front.

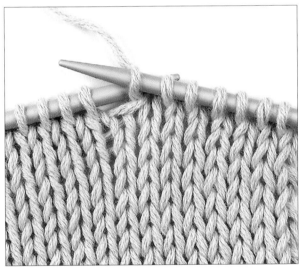

8. Turn work, slip first stitch as if to purl (wrap made), complete row.

9. To work stitch and wrap together from wrong side, insert tip of right needle under wrap from right side and place it on left needle.

10. Purl stitch and wrap together. (Wrap will automatically fall on wrong side of fabric.)

11. This is a photo of a wrapped stitch on right side.

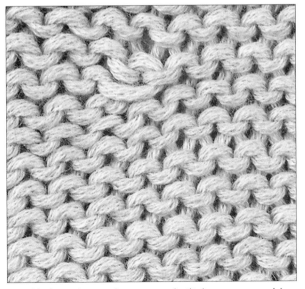

12. This is a photo of a wrapped stitch on wrong side.

Slip Stitch (Sl st)

A slip stitch is passed from the left needle to the right needle without being worked. Unless you are instructed otherwise, stitches are usually slipped as if you're purling, with the yarn on the wrong side of the fabric. Slipped stitches are part of a number of knitting techniques, including texture and color patterns such as mosaic knitting.

1. Insert tip of right needle in next stitch as if to purl. Slide stitch off left needle onto right needle.

Yarn Over (yo)

A yarn over creates an intentional hole in a piece of knitting. It may be used to increase the number of stitches (for example, shaping a shawl) or paired with a corresponding decrease to create openwork or lace patterns. This example shows a yo between two knit stitches.

1. Bring yarn to front and over top of right needle.

2. Knit the next stitch.

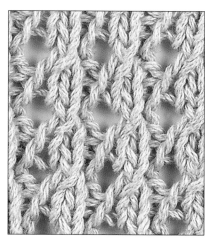

3. Here is an example of a delicate lace pattern that can be created with yarn overs.

Slip Knot

The slip knot forms the first stitch of a cast on. Knit Tip: Remember to keep the short end or tail facing you, the knitter.

1. Form overhand knot.

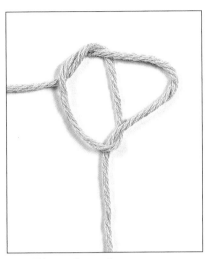

2. Pull loop through.

3. Tighten on needle.

Long Tail Cast On

This cast-on technique is a very useful beginning, worked with one needle and two strands. It is strong, forms an attractive edge and is best followed with a wrong side row. Knit Tip: Estimate the length of the tail by allowing approximately three times the width of the finished piece, plus 4 to 6 inches so you have a nice end for finishing. Begin with a slip knot on the needle.

1. Holding needle in right hand, place left thumb and forehand between strands of yarn, catching ends of strands with remaining fingers. Remember to keep the tail over the thumb. Insert tip of needle in front of thumb loop.

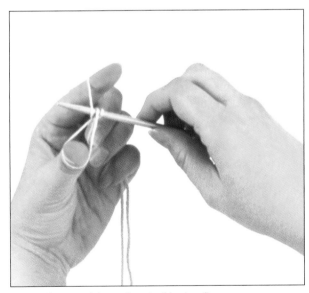

2. Catch strand from front of index finger.

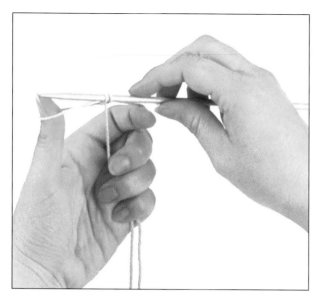

3. Pull strand through thumb loop.

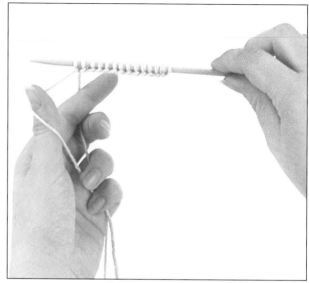

5. Repeat steps 1 through 4 until desired number of stitches has been cast on. When you count your stitches, do not forget to count the slip knot.

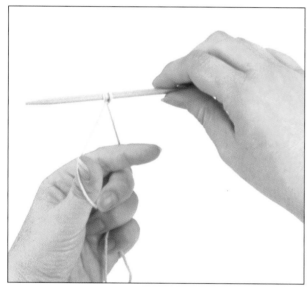

4. Remove thumb from loop and pull stitch snug, but not too tight.

Knitting Basics

Cable Cast-On

This type of cast-on is used when adding stitches in the middle or at the end of a row.

Make a slip knot on the left needle.

Knit a stitch in this knot and place it on the left needle.

Insert the right needle between the last two stitches on the left needle. Knit a stitch and place it on the left needle. Repeat for each stitch needed.

Knit (K)

Insert tip of right needle from front to back in next stitch on left needle.

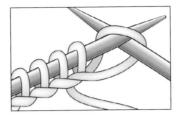

Bring yarn under and over the tip of the right needle.

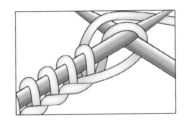

Pull yarn loop through the stitch with right needle point.

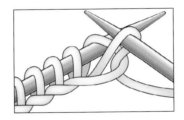

Slide the stitch off the left needle. The new stitch is on the right needle.

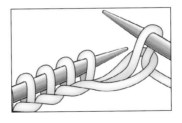

Purl (P)

With yarn in front, insert tip of right needle from back to front through next stitch on the left needle.

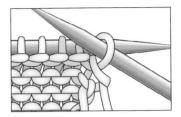

Bring yarn around the right needle counterclockwise.

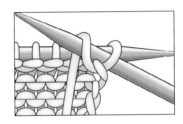

With right needle, draw yarn back through the stitch.

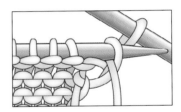

Slide the stitch off the left needle. The new stitch is on the right needle.

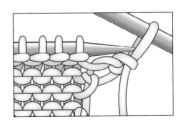

Bind Off

Binding off (knit)

Knit first two stitches on left needle. Insert tip of left needle into first stitch worked on right needle and pull it over the second stitch and completely off the needle.

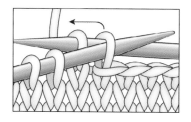

Knit the next stitch and repeat. When one stitch remains on right needle, cut yarn and draw tail through last stitch to fasten off.

Binding off (purl)

Purl first two stitches on left needle. Insert tip of left needle into first stitch worked on right needle and pull it over the second stitch and completely off the needle.

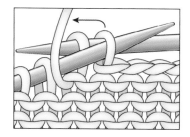

Purl the next stitch and repeat. When one stitch remains on right needle, cut yarn and draw tail through last stitch to fasten off.

Increase (Inc)
Two stitches in one stitch
Increase (knit)

Knit the next stitch in the usual manner, but don't remove the stitch from the left needle. Place right needle behind left needle and knit again into the back of the same stitch. Slip original stitch off left needle.

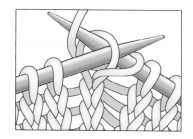

Increase (purl)

Purl the next stitch in the usual manner, but don't remove the stitch from the left needle. Place right needle behind left needle and purl again into the back of the same stitch. Slip original stitch off left needle.

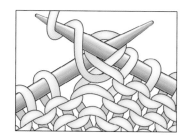

Make 1 Increase (M1)

Invisible Increase

Insert left needle from front to back under the horizontal loop between the last stitch worked and next stitch on left needle.

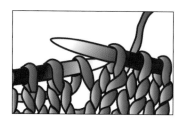

With right needle, knit into the back of this loop.

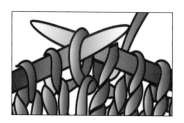

Backward Loop Increase over the right needle

With your thumb, make a loop over the right needle.

Slip the loop from your thumb onto the needle and pull to tighten.

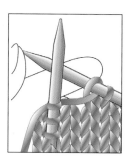

Make 1 Increase in top of stitch below

Insert tip of right needle into the stitch on left needle one row below.

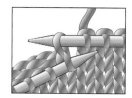

Knit this stitch, then knit the stitch on the left needle.

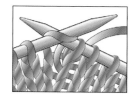

Decrease (Dec)

Knit 2 together (k2tog)
Put tip of right needle through next two stitches on left needle as to knit. Knit these two stitches as one.

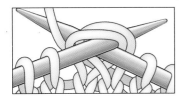

Purl 2 together (p2tog)
Put tip of right needle through next two stitches on left needle as to purl. Purl these two stitches as one.

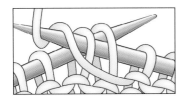

Slip, Slip, Knit (ssk)

Slip next two stitches, one at a time, as if to knit from left needle to right needle.

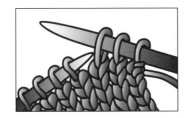

Insert left needle in front of both stitches and work off needle together.

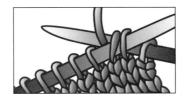

Slip, Slip, Purl (ssp)

Slip next two stitches, one at a time, as if to knit from left needle to right needle. Slip these stitches back onto left needle keeping them twisted.

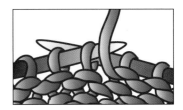

Purl these two stitches together through back loops.

Crochet Basics

Some knit items are finished with a crochet trim or edging. Below are some abbreviations used in crochet and a review of some basic crochet stitches.

CROCHET ABBREVIATIONS
ch	chain stitch
dc	double crochet
hdc	half double crochet
lp(s)	loop(s)
sc	single crochet
sl st	slip stitch
yo	yarn over

Chain Stitch (ch)
Begin by making a slip knot on the hook. Bring the yarn over the hook from back to front and draw through the loop on the hook.

For each additional chain stitch, bring the yarn over the hook from back to front and draw through the loop on the hook.

Single Crochet (sc)
Insert the hook in the second chain through the center of the V. Bring the yarn over the hook from back to front.

Draw the yarn through the chain stitch and onto the hook.

Again bring yarn over the hook from back to front and draw it through both loops on hook.

For additional rows of single crochet, insert the hook under both loops of the previous stitch instead of through the center of the V as when working into the chain stitch.

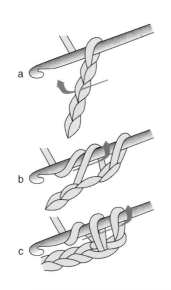

Reverse Single Crochet (reverse sc)

Working in opposite direction from single crochet, insert hook under both loops of the next stitch to the right.

Bring yarn over hook from back to front and draw through both loops on hook.

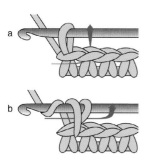

Half-Double Crochet (hdc)

Bring yarn over hook from back to front, insert hook in indicated chain stitch.

Draw yarn through the chain stitch and onto the hook.

Bring yarn over the hook from back to front and draw it through all three loops on the hook in one motion.

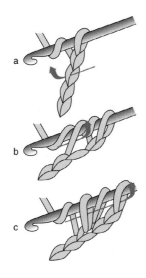

Double Crochet (dc)

Yo, insert hook in st, yo, pull through st, (yo, pull through 2 lps) 2 times.

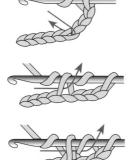

Treble Crochet (tr)

Yo 2 times, insert hook in st, yo, pull through st, (yo, pull through 2 lps) 3 times.

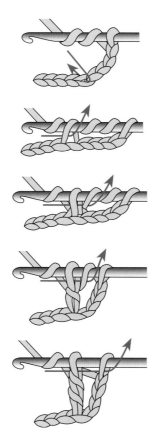

Slip Stitch (sl st)

Insert hook under both loops of the stitch, bring yarn over the hook from back to front and draw it through the stitch and the loop on the hook.

Picot

Picots can be made in a variety of ways so refer to pattern for specific instructions.

Chain required number of stitches. Insert hook at base of chain stitches and through back loop of stitch, complete as indicated in pattern.

INCHES INTO MILLIMETERS & CENTIMETERS (Rounded off slightly)

inches	mm	cm	inches	cm	inches	cm	inches	cm
1/8	3	0.3	5	12.5	21	53.5	38	96.5
1/4	6	0.6	5 1/2	14	22	56	39	99
3/8	10	1	6	15	23	58.5	40	101.5
1/2	13	1.3	7	18	24	61	41	104
5/8	15	1.5	8	20.5	25	63.5	42	106.5
3/4	20	2	9	23	26	66	43	109
7/8	22	2.2	10	25.5	27	68.5	44	112
1	25	2.5	11	28	28	71	45	114.5
1 1/4	32	3.2	12	30.5	29	73.5	46	117
1 1/2	38	3.8	13	33	30	76	47	119.5
1 3/4	45	4.5	14	35.5	31	79	48	122
2	50	5	15	38	32	81.5	49	124.5
2 1/2	65	6.5	16	40.5	33	84	50	127
3	75	7.5	17	43	34	86.5		
3 1/2	90	9	18	46	35	89		
4	100	10	19	48.5	36	91.5		
4 1/2	115	11.5	20	51	37	94		

KNITTING NEEDLES CONVERSION CHART

U.S.	0	1	2	3	4	5	6	7	8	9	10	10 1/2	11	13	15
Metric(mm)	2	2 1/4	2 3/4	3 1/4	3 1/2	3 3/4	4	4 1/2	5	5 1/2	6	6 1/2	8	9	10

CROCHET HOOKS CONVERSION CHART

U.S.	1/B	2/C	3/D	4/E	5/F	6/G	8/H	9/I	10/J	10 1/2/K	N
Continental(mm)	2.25	2.75	3.25	3.5	3.75	4.25	5	5.5	6	6.5	9.0

Standard Yarn Weight System

Categories of yarn, gauge ranges, and recommended needle sizes

Yarn Weight Symbol & Category Names	1 SUPER FINE	2 FINE	3 LIGHT	4 MEDIUM	5 BULKY	6 SUPER BULKY
Type of Yarns in Category	Sock, Fingering, Baby	Sport, Baby	DK, Light Worsted	Worsted, Afghan, Aran	Chunky, Craft, Rug	Bulky, Roving
Knit Gauge* Ranges in Stockinette Stitch to 4 inches	21–32 sts	23–26 sts	21–24 sts	16–20 sts	12–15 sts	6–11 sts
Recommended Needle in Metric Size Range	2.25–3.25mm	3.25–3.75mm	3.75–4.5mm	4.5–5.5mm	5.5–8mm	8mm
Recommended Needle U.S. Size Range	1 to 3	3 to 5	5 to 7	7 to 9	9 to 11	11 and larger

* GUIDELINES ONLY: The above reflect the most commonly used gauges and needle sizes for specific yarn categories.

SPECIAL THANKS

We would like to thank Plymouth Yarn Co. for providing all the yarn used in this book. We especially appreciate the help provided by JoAnne Turcotte. It's been great working with her. We would also like to thank the talented knitting designers whose work is featured in this collection.